Retirement Fail

Retirement Fail

THE 9 REASONS PEOPLE FLUNK POST-WORK LIFE—AND HOW TO ACE YOUR OWN

Greg Sullivan, CPA, CFP®

**President and CEO,
Sullivan, Bruyette, Speros & Blayney, LLC**

WILEY

Published by John Wiley & Sons, Inc., Hoboken, New Jersey.

Published simultaneously in Canada.

For general information on our other products and services or for technical support, please contact our Customer Care Department within the United States at (800) 762–2974, outside the United States at (317) 572–3993, or fax (317) 572–4002.

Wiley publishes in a variety of print and electronic formats and by print-on-demand. Some material included with standard print versions of this book may not be included in e-books or in print-on-demand. If this book refers to media such as a CD or DVD that is not included in the version you purchased, you may download this material at http://booksupport.wiley.com. For more information about Wiley products, visit www.wiley.com.

Library of Congress Cataloging-in-Publication Data is Available:

ISBN 9781119447405 (Hardcover)
ISBN 9781119452966 (ePDF)
ISBN 9781119452980 (ePub)

Cover Design: Wiley

Printed in the United States of America.

10 9 8 7 6 5 4 3 2 1

Disclosure

The stories in *Retirement Fail* are based on actual scenarios and events; however, names and identifying details may have been changed to protect the privacy of those discussed. In some instances, composites have been created.

This book is offered as a resource for informational purposes only. The information is being presented without consideration of the investment objectives, risk tolerance, or financial circumstances of any specific investor and may not be suitable for all investors. Always consult your own financial, legal, and/or tax advisor before making any decisions related to your investment, tax, estate, or financial planning.

To Mom and Dad

For their love and guidance

Contents

Acknowledgments   ix

Introduction   xiii

Chapter 1   A (Too) Free Flow of Cash   1

Chapter 2   The Nest That Won't Empty   20

Chapter 3   Graying Divorce   36

Chapter 4   That Home Away from Home   55

Chapter 5   The Lure of the Entrepreneur   69

Chapter 6   Swindler's Mark   85

Chapter 7   Health Matters   99

Chapter 8   Life's Unpredictabilities   114

Chapter 9   Underliving Your Wealth   136

Finding the Right Financial Advisor   144

Checklist: Finding the Right Advisor   149

About the Author   **151**

Resources   **152**

Notes   **153**

Index   **159**

Acknowledgments

To ace retirement and not fail requires discipline, effort, a little luck, and a lot of wise guidance along the way. The same goes for writing a book. That is why I am so thankful for all the people who have guided, taught, and influenced me during this journey.

My Mom and Dad had the greatest influence on me, encouraging me in ways they may never know. I reference them in the book many times because I learned so much from watching the way they handled tough times and good times, both personally and financially, and talked openly about money and finance while I was growing up. So, Mom and Dad, a big thank-you for your guidance, unconditional love, and support.

I am fortunate to have great siblings and a fabulous brother-in-law, and we are all so close that they allowed me to share stories about them. I know they are very thankful for the stories I left out! Thank you Gail, Bill, Pam, and my brother-in-law Frank, for always being there for me!

Twenty-seven years ago, three men and a lady decided it was time to start a business that focused on providing objective, independent advice to individuals and families without the concern of self-dealing and conflicts of interest. We all took a leap of faith – a lot of faith, because our new job couldn't afford to pay us a salary – but we had a strong belief that we would change the way people receive financial advice, and we aced it! To Jim Bruyette, Pete Speros, and Eleanor Blayney, I will forever be grateful for your leadership and for being patient with me. Most importantly, thank you for making this journey so much fun and for your friendship, which I will always treasure.

At SBSB we have an amazing team of professionals, and this book would not have come to be without the help and inspiration of the whole group. Together as a team, we make a difference in our clients' lives and in the lives of one another. You have all been a part of the stories in this book and the millions more that I haven't written about. To our entire team at SBSB, I want to say thank you for your passion for excellence and your amazing desire to serve our clients with the utmost integrity and respect.

I want to give special thanks to several SBSB partners and colleagues: Kris Andrejev, Jim Bruyette, Patrick Dunne, Gary Ingram, Martine Lellis, Jeff Porter, Barbara Schelhorn, Pete Speros, and Karen Tovey. These advisors gave freely of their time (often their lunch hours) and expertise, agreeing to be interviewed, sharing their experience, and providing indispensible context for the book.

Friends and colleagues in related businesses also offered critical background and shared their stories of attending to clients' special insurance needs. Thank you to Diane Beatty, Virg Cristobal, Stafford Jacobs, Jon Katz, and Kim Natovitz for your generosity in sharing your stories and advice. And a special thank-you to Mark Tibergien, a great friend and mentor, whose wisdom and guidance over the past twenty-five years has been invaluable. Thank you, Mark, for introducing me to Wiley and for your keen insights for this book.

We are so blessed at SBSB to have clients who care about us as much as we care about them. Although it is not appropriate to name any of them here, I want to thank our clients for making this book possible. The stories we share make the situations real and provide tremendous guidance and insight that others can learn from. Thank you to all our clients, who make going to work every day a true joy.

In writing this book I was thinking about how to help people open up and have conversations with their partners and their advisors in areas that are often sensitive, and to provide stories and content that was relevant to creating a successful retirement. I wasn't thinking about marketing. Fortunately, I have Katie King, Caitlin Norton, and Jeanne Rossomme to think about that for me. Your ideas have helped me understand how to share the book and the stories through social media and other means. Thank you for all the guidance and advice on how to get the word out and for your thoughtful comments on the book's cover and the initial manuscript.

One of the core values at SBSB is "Lifetime of Learning." Out of necessity, in the early 1980s, much of the learning was OJT (on-the-job training). But there was also a group of advisors, passionate about financial planning, who met regularly to share ideas and learn from one another. We eventually formalized the group and named it the Alpha Group. I am proud to say the group today includes many of the most respected and influential leaders in the wealth management profession. A couple of us then brought together a group of leading CEOs in the field and created the Blind Squirrels, a group of entrepreneurs focusing on all aspects of building a great business. The value these two groups brought to me and our profession is immense. Thank you all for sharing your wisdom and experience. I learned from you how to be a better advisor, leader, and CEO.

This book would never have made it to reality if it weren't for Caitlin Norton and Susan Lauzau. I gave Caitlin a tough task: Help me find an experienced professional who knows the book writing world and who can guide me and help me turn my ideas and stories into a book people will enjoy reading. Caitlin did her research and introduced me to Susan Lauzau, a fabulous writer, talented editor, and genuinely humble person. Susan, you have a special gift for creativity and a wonderful ability to endure my endless ideas, changes, and rewrites. You helped make this book real and fun to read. Thank you for keeping me on task and on time. Thank you, too, for your invaluable guidance and for making this an amazing journey.

My kids, David and Lisa, bring me incredible love and joy, and I want to thank them for letting me share a few stories about them in the book. What child wants their dad writing about them and publishing it to the world? Thank you, David and Lisa, for being amazing kids, for all the great adventures we have been on together, for the challenges we have faced together, and most importantly for being my best friends.

Writing a book over an extended twelve-month period while running a rapidly growing company full time requires a lot of TLC and patience. Not from me, but from my loving and caring wife, Pam. Thank you, Pam, for being simply fabulous and wonderful and patient with me throughout this process. Thank you for reading and rereading the many drafts. Thank you for encouraging me along the way and for your love and support. Despite all the hard work over the past twelve months, we still managed to have a lot of fun! I love you.

Introduction

What causes a retirement fail? That is, why do people who have prepared for retirement end up unable to fully enjoy the thing they worked so hard for? I have thought about this question a lot. Most people believe that it's due to poor investments. But I cannot recall a single instance in which investment performance has been the cause of a client losing financial independence or failing to enjoy the life in retirement that he or she desired.

I joke with my clients that, rather than portfolio performance, it's usually the things you have to care for that weigh more than 50 pounds that wreak havoc on retirement finances: Grown kids, houses, horses, cars, boats. Clients laugh with me, sometimes because they have already made these mistakes – or, more often, because they are wondering which decisions down the road will impact their own retirement. What do you think can trip you up in your post-work life? Will it be your finances, health, family, a divorce, a scam? The list goes on.

Retirement Fail is not about going broke or becoming destitute; it is about the personal, emotional, and financial decisions you make that can disrupt the life you could have enjoyed in your post-work life. Whether you have $500,000, $5 million, or $50 million, the issues we discuss are real and relevant, not only for you but for your children and other family members.

I talk with my clients about how to plan for the *evitable*, for the things you are capable of avoiding. People focus on the *inevitable* – what will happen, no matter what – and that's important, too. But we humans may be tempted to throw up our hands and leave to chance the very things we truly can control, those we should be taking thoughtful and deliberate steps to avoid. We sometimes court retirement fail.

A Kernel of an Idea

In the fall of 2014, Evan Simonoff, editor-in-chief and editorial director of *Financial Advisor* magazine as well as editorial director of *Private Wealth* magazine, called me and asked me to speak at the Inside Retirement Conference, which focuses on current topics that affect retirees. He asked if I could speak on using income-generating assets for retirement in a low-interest-rate environment. "That is a great topic," I told Evan, "but what I would love to talk about is how people fail in retirement." No one is talking about this issue, I told him, though 10,000 people are retiring every day. I shared that I had nine reasons I have seen people fail in retirement, and that the best way to avoid those failures was to get the conversation going early. Evan didn't hesitate for a second: "I love it . . . that's your subject," he told me.

Every day, I and my colleagues at Sullivan, Bruyette, Speros & Blayney (SBSB) talk with our clients about decision making in retirement and in the lead-up years. And while we discuss investments, how to best allocate portfolios for cash needs, taxes, and other related items, most of our energy goes into discussions that are far thornier. These conversations can be delicate because they often involve a person's most deep-rooted wishes, fears, or insecurities: Maintaining his or her role as provider for the kids (even though the children are in their 30s); recovering one's identity after exiting the professional world by starting a business (even a high-risk business like a trendy restaurant or a vineyard); or buying that dream vacation home (even though it might not be truly affordable).

The topic struck a nerve – the room was packed, and other advisors came up to me after the conference, wanting to learn more about how to have these important discussions with *their* clients. Evan later wrote a piece for *Financial Advisor* based on my talk and our conversations, and that, too, generated a lot of buzz and comments from other financial advisors. And the more I thought about it, the more I realized how critical the emotional part of retirement planning and decision making truly is, and how much my clients and others like them could benefit from a guide to take away, with stories that underlined the realities of some common retirement fails.

Are You Talking to Me?

There are plenty of books about how much money you need in retirement and how to save and invest your cash. This is not one of them.

I wrote *Retirement Fail* for those of you who have been preparing for retirement financially but need some guidance to ensure that your plans for a happy, healthy retirement are not compromised. Ready or not, you will be making decisions that can positively or negatively impact your financial future. You may be on track with savings goals, but there are potential pitfalls ahead, and the deepest pits are the ones you don't even see or, in some cases, those you would rather not acknowledge.

Many people have good, strong financial plans, but they don't necessarily notice themselves getting caught up in troubling patterns – or they may be surprised by an event they didn't see coming. The numerical side is one thing; an advisor can easily come up with numbers and projections. The more difficult thing is to look at the way the decisions we all make impact our own future and those around us. *Retirement Fail* shows you the watch points you need to pay attention to and helps you think through what your priorities are – and what trade-offs you may have to make to reach your goals.

If you're working with a financial advisor – and a Certified Financial Planner Board of Standards (CFP Board) survey indicates that 40% of Americans are now consulting a financial professional[1] – you can use this book to help start productive conversations with your advisor. You don't need to stick to the technical investments and hard numbers – as you'll see from the stories in *Retirement Fail,* we see lots of different scenarios and can offer suggestions for handling many complex issues related to individual and family finances.

We like to share stories, both those of clients (all carefully anonymous, of course) and from our own lives. Money is one of those things people often don't talk about with their friends. That's why stories are so powerful – it's why we use them in our meetings and why I use them throughout this book. We can say, "We know another person who was in your exact spot, and this is what he did." Everybody likes confirmation or affirmation that they are making wise decisions, or that others faced similar situations and came out on the other side. We can learn from others' successes and take warning from their losses.

Where's the Advice?

My parents dropped me off at the main campus of Penn State University in September 1975. I was surrounded by mountains (locals call the area Happy Valley) and by 30,000 other eager, energetic college students. Mom and Dad took me out for lunch before they left, and my dad asked me what I thought I was going to do when I graduated.

That was an interesting question for a freshman who had not yet been to one class. But I was one of those rare freshmen who actually did have an idea of what I wanted to do. I had loved reading about stocks and different businesses since I was young, so I said, "I am either going to work on Wall Street and help people with their finances or I am going to be CEO of a company and run a business." Without skipping a beat, he said, "The smartest people I know in business are CPAs [certified public accountants]. You should get a degree in accounting." Being a bean counter had never crossed my mind – I wanted to help people with their finances and investments.

My father's words stuck with me, though, and when I graduated with a degree in accounting I went to work for Ernst & Whinney (now Ernst & Young) in Washington, DC. After a couple of years in public accounting, I left and joined a local brokerage firm as a financial planner, following my real passion.

Excited about the job change, I called my parents to tell them of my big move. Dad, a bit shocked, said, "Why would you leave a great career in public accounting to become a salesman?" When I told him I was going to be a financial planner, not a salesman, he replied, "Every financial planner I know is just trying to sell me something."

I thought he didn't know what he was talking about. I had this vision of helping people, not selling to them. But darned if he wasn't right. A few months after I started my job, I went to the national financial planning conference. There were several thousand attendees, and everyone I met was selling something: Insurance, annuities, heavy commission-based mutual funds, private partnerships, and so on. Where was the advice? Who was helping people make smart financial decisions?

I was fortunate in my new job, and one colleague in particular, the late Dave Dondero, took me under his wing and helped me learn how to prepare a financial plan driven by a client's goals and financial capabilities. I taught classes, wrote case studies, and became the in-house expert on tax and financial planning strategies. Most of the people at the company used my work to sell products, but I was learning the craft and building a reputation for providing quality advice.

In 1988 I decided to start my own independent firm, Sullivan Financial Consultants, with the goal of helping clients make smart financial decisions, untroubled by conflicts of interest. Then, in 1991, I was fortunate to partner in a new enterprise with Jim Bruyette, a former colleague of mine from Ernst & Whinney, Pete

Speros, and Eleanor Blayney. We all shared the same passion – to help clients make smart financial decisions and to be independent and conflict free. We would provide the advice. We would help people make sound decisions about their finances.

Which brings me back around to the reason I wrote this book – and, more importantly, to the reason you are reading it. At the heart of retirement planning is the question: What is most important to you in your post-work life and how can you translate that into your day-to-day living and decision making? Once you know the answer to that question, you can frame your decisions so that your assets are truly working for you and your spending is aligned with your values and objectives. *Retirement Fail* helps you answer that essential question, addressing the nine ways you are most likely to compromise your retirement (and visit RetirementFail.com for more information and tips to help you succeed as you move into your post-work life). Armed with a sense of your values and goals – and a true awareness of the challenges that may lie ahead – you can craft a plan that lets you ace your retirement.

Retirement Fail

CHAPTER 1

A (Too) Free Flow of Cash

I was talking to a client who was living the good life in Florida. Julia owned a beautiful penthouse condominium, drove a sporty car, traveled frequently with friends, and wore ultra-stylish clothing. Looking at her, you would have thought everything in her life was going well. Underneath the surface, however, lay the nagging question of whether Julia's assets could support her extravagant lifestyle forever. Condominium fees and real estate taxes were upward of $100,000 per year, and her travel expenses typically amounted to about $10,000 per month. She was enjoying life, and why not? This was the way she had lived when she was married, so why should things change?

In her divorce, Julia received a generous settlement, which included her luxury condominium. Of course, she felt her home needed to be thoroughly renovated postdivorce, to reflect her new outlook on life. Essentially, Julia was spending money like she had no financial constraints whatsoever. The divorce agreement did not include lifetime spousal support, however, so she needed to make sure she could live on the assets she received in the settlement.

After a candid conversation with Julia, I realized that she needed help organizing her finances and then gaining control over her spending. She needed some guidelines for setting an appropriate monthly spending limit for herself.

My suggestion that Julia downsize her home to get out from under the large housing expense did not go over well initially. But she came to understand the potential crisis looming and began looking at other housing options. That was the first and most important step: Getting her to recognize that her spending issue was real and that she needed to change certain habits if she wanted

1

to continue enjoying some of the other things that were important to her, such as traveling. Sometimes we have to start with baby steps, even when a big change is ultimately required.

As financial advisors, we see situations like Julia's – in which people are living a lifestyle that outstrips their means – more often than you might imagine. You read celebrity versions of these stories in the press sometimes. The front page will be emblazoned with a headline about a major sports star or movie actor who retired several years earlier and now is declaring bankruptcy. From Jerry Lee Lewis to Gary Coleman to Lenny Dykstra, we've seen dozens of formerly wealthy celebrities file for bankruptcy over the years. Because these celebrities made millions of dollars at the pinnacle of their careers, they think they are eternally rich and can live the high life forever. They forget that their stratospheric income is no longer coming in and they need to live off the assets they've already accumulated.

Your Retirement Spending Picture

How do you envision your life as you grow older and begin working less or retire altogether? Will you travel the world on luxury cruises? Spend half of every year on the white sands that stretch in front of your new beachfront home or Caribbean bungalow? Or perhaps you plan to buy that picturesque horse farm you've always yearned for and occupy your time cultivating the next Derby winner. If you've built up your wealth and planned for this future, these dreams may well be within reach. But it's also possible that unrestrained spending could lead you down a path that will ultimately crack your nest egg. Which scenario comes to pass depends not only on your level of wealth and on how many hefty expenditures you make, but on what you want to accomplish in retirement and the trade-offs you are willing to make to achieve your goals.

Imprudent spending is one major reason people fail at retirement – and it lies at the root of many of the other potential pitfalls I talk about in this book, from the purchase of vacation homes to overgenerous support for adult children. So how can you tell the difference between a luxury (or a lifestyle) you can happily afford – or are willing to make reasonable trade-offs for – and an indulgence that will ultimately undermine your retirement goals? What separates a hard-won dream from a serious mistake? Before we can examine overspending, we have to look at broader spending philosophies and at some of the ways that spending in retirement differs from outlays you make while you are still working at full capacity.

When evaluating retirement plans, nearly everything centers around spending, either directly or indirectly. Most people are, in fact, overly cautious, so the number of people who jeopardize their retirement due to extravagant purchases is not large by percentage; but overspending is a significant problem for those who have it. And sometimes a pattern of free spending is enough to raise caution flags, even if no single expenditure is outsized.

When you are working full time and have a healthy income, it is easy to develop lavish spending habits. Nice vacations, meals out at upscale restaurants, frequent shopping trips, and other treats are among the ways people reward themselves for a productive week's work and cope with the stresses that come with a busy life. In retirement, people may have the same desires for material possessions and entertainment that they had before they stopped working, but now they have more time – more time to travel, more time to shop, more time to pursue potentially expensive hobbies or interests like collecting cars, starting a winery, enjoying multiple homes, or indulging in large-scale boating. And in retirement, their income is a fraction of what it once was, so it's easy to overspend assets.

While conventional wisdom dictates that people need 80% of their preretirement income to maintain their lifestyle in their post-work years, recent research has shown that spending patterns are actually quite variable – while some households do indeed reduce their spending considerably, nearly half spent more in the first two years of retirement than they had while working.[1] And 28% of the retirees surveyed spent more than 120% of what they'd spent in the years preceding retirement, with the majority continuing that pattern of increased spending into their sixth year of retirement.[2] So, while 80% may indeed represent an average, the spending picture is uneven, with some households cutting spending by a sizable amount and others actually increasing their outlays rather dramatically. According to the data, most of the increased spending was discretionary in nature, used either for travel or for home expenses.

In retirement, you may not be taking a hard enough look at your household spending. As an executive you might have been brilliant at developing business strategy, assessing corporate cash flow, and understanding the company's financial health, but it's possible that you do not take the same clear-eyed view of your own finances.

It's much more difficult to see your personal spending rationally, particularly when what you *should* do and what you *want* to do are in conflict.

In the corporate world, you are playing with other people's money; when it comes to personal finance, you are, of course, dealing with your own, and your spouse has a say in how the money is being spent. Once you're retired, you are unlikely to be adding to your retirement bucket. You have a finite amount of assets to draw from over an uncertain period of time. For most people, living within one's means requires careful thought and planning.

We find that, for most people, managing their personal finances has never been their strong suit. If you are a person whose career success has come in law, business, sports, or entrepreneurship – or if your money has come to you through an inheritance – you may not be attuned to the details of cash inflows versus outflows and how they relate to your lifestyle and investment assets. You were bringing in more than enough money, so there was no need to pay close attention to what was gushing out.

When you are used to having money in the bank, you may be inattentive to your spending habits. And as long as cash is coming in at a brisk rate, that approach may work. But what happens when your income slows or stops, either because you've decided to retire or because your circumstances change? How will you make the transition from an income based on full-time work to an income based primarily on your investment assets' performance, which is often much less than what you'd been bringing in? How will you decide what "appropriate" or "lavish" spending is, and how will you reset your habits if you need to?

Priorities, and Who Decides Them

One of the difficulties is determining who decides what lavish spending is. Is it the husband or the wife? Do the in-laws, children, friends, or neighbors influence spending decisions? It is easy for people to make judgments about excessive spending when critiquing another individual or family – typically, the definition of *excessive* is "more than I would spend" on any given item or category.

But people see life differently, and their priorities and spending patterns often originate in their upbringing. Growing up in a family that was either financially stressed or spent extravagantly, hearing frequent parental arguments about finances, and suffering childhood trauma of various types can lead to a complicated or unhealthy relationship with money. Sometimes a person's individual temperament and/or the financial behaviors he or she learned growing up contribute to spending patterns that later cause conflict with a spouse.

Husbands and wives very often have different money personalities. They simply look at money and what it means differently. One spouse might think buying a new car every three or four years is unnecessary and wasteful, while the other considers it a normal and appropriate expense. One partner might view the kids' private school tuition as an extravagance, while the other sees it as an essential investment in their children's future. Who decides, and what impact will those decisions have on the couple's retirement goals?

According to a 2016 Ameriprise survey, approximately 31% of couples disagree about finances at least once a month. The most common points of disagreement are major purchases (34%), decisions about finance and children (24% of respondents who have children), a partner's spending habits (23%), and important investment decisions (14%).[3]

I was working with a husband and wife, Mark and Teri, both of whom had great jobs, but, based on our financial analysis, were not saving appropriately for their retirement. These two were setting aside money in their 401(k) plans but, given their income level, they needed to save a lot more if they wanted to generate a retirement income in line with their lifestyle.

The biggest obstacle to saving was that Mark and Teri had two children in private middle school at a cost of $30,000 per year, per child. That meant they needed $60,000 in after-tax dollars for tuition. In their tax bracket, the first $110,000 of their income ($60,000 after taxes) was going toward schooling – and this expense was going to continue for five more years before the children were off to college. And, of course, it was likely these kids would be attending private colleges at more than $50,000 per year, per child.

I knew that the neighborhood the family lived in had fabulous public schools because my children attended those schools. So we explored why these parents felt the need to have their kids in private middle school, potentially disrupting or delaying the couple's own future retirement. As we discussed the matter, it became clear that Mark felt they had to "keep up with the Joneses." They were running with a well-heeled crowd, and he felt the need to say, "My children go to the Potomac School" (a very prestigious school in our area).

While the school was, no question, a fine one, Mark's pride was the real issue: Sending one's children to that particular school was a notable status symbol. Teri, a successful attorney, had grown up in a middle-class neighborhood and attended public schools. She went along with the decision, even though she was concerned about the cost.

Many couples face dilemmas similar to Mark and Teri's, and they are not easy ones to solve – especially when two equally worthy goals are competing, such as a solid education for the kids and an ample retirement portfolio for the parents (setting aside here any status-seeking motives). Neither partner is right or wrong when it comes to these spending decisions.

Appropriate spending comes down to priorities and to what is reasonable given your personal finances, values, and goals. If you have a goal of retiring at age 60 or 65, you must consider: Does this particular decision draw you closer to your goal? If the answer is no, you have to ask, is this expenditure worth what I must trade for it? For example, is a private education for your children (or your grand-children) such a high priority and core value for you that you are okay delaying retirement? Either yes or no may be the right answer for you; it all depends on what you want to do with your money and the sacrifices you are able and willing to make.

For every financial decision, you have a choice: Save or spend. For each major spending decision, ask: Does this expenditure reflect what is important to us? What is the impact of the decision on those around us? Will our personal finances support this decision? Does the decision support our family's values? Are we moving closer to our personal goals with this decision?

In Mark and Teri's case, spending on tuition created stress for Teri, but Mark felt strongly that they were making the right deci-sion and should stick with it. As we dug a little deeper, we learned that Mark had an unspoken backup plan. He talked about a poten-tial and likely inheritance from his parents, which he anticipated would fully replace the education costs and adequately fund their retirement account. The actual inheritance would likely be a long way down the line – and wasn't a certainty – but the probability that they'd inherit a sizable amount allowed him to sleep at night. Mark and Teri elected to keep their kids in private school, and we agreed to review education costs and retirement needs annually.

Setting Goals

Take some time to reflect on your goals for this next phase of your life, a period when you have either stopped working or have slowed markedly. How will you spend your time? What kind of lifestyle do you expect to have? What will your days look like? Tally all the things you'd like to do in a typical year, and also the things you'd like to do for family. Think ahead, too, to how your life might change as you age, and make provisions for unforeseen events.

Researchers have discovered that, though people may have a realistic understanding of how much income they have, they have blind spots when it comes to forecasting expenses.[4] They focus on what is coming in and underestimate what is going out, which leads them to be overly optimistic about what they can afford. Talk about your projected expenses with your financial advisor. Get a second opinion and some feedback. Financial advisors deal with income versus spending issues all the time, so we have many experiences to draw from to help you find the right path for you and your family.

A strong financial plan takes into account your monthly expenses such as housing, food, entertainment, and health insurance; savings for purchases such as a new car or for major home repairs; extra expenses you want to budget for in retirement such as travel or home health care; and taxes you will need to pay. You should also think about other things you may wish to pay for, such as contributions to an adult child's wedding, a child's medical school tuition, or a grandchild's college bills. Once you have a firm sense of what your projected outlays are, you will be able to think about the other things you want to do and how they will impact your overall plan.

I remember receiving a call from a client who said he needed to pull $35,000 from his account for an unexpected expense; his roof had a major leak and needed to be replaced. I asked how old the roof was, and he said, "Twenty-five years." I wondered if this expense was "unexpected" because it occurred in July or because he thought the roof would never need to be replaced! Make sure to plan for those nonrecurring expenses such as home and auto repairs, along with recurring expenses.

What we are really talking about when we discuss goal setting and spending plans are the trade-offs you need to make in life, reflected in the way you spend the income or assets you have today. A spending plan, in essence, codifies what is important to you and helps you think through the impact of the decisions you make. Your choice always comes down to this: Spend now or save for future goals.

Have you ever made a major spending decision and then looked back on it a few years later and wondered, "What was I thinking?" So often, spending makes you feel good. It is incredibly rewarding... until you think about your purchase a few months or years later. You probably make more of these questionable decisions than you realize: Joining the country club, buying the boat, splurging on a blowout wedding for your daughter, buying the second home, making major charitable gifts or family gifts. The particular decisions you make about finances are less important than the practice of evaluating what you want to do and setting a spending plan that aligns with your values and your financial goals.

The challenge also comes when you can't seem to say no to anyone, knocking your spending out of alignment with your stated financial capabilities. Your child asks for financial help to support a personal need, the church asks for additional donations, a friend suggests a wonderful trip that your families should take together, your spouse is excited to buy this new boat that will bring the family together on weekends, and so on. But will saying yes to all of these things get you closer to your objective? It is the nature of priorities that not everything can be at the top of the list.

Funneling Your Wealth to Meet Your Goals

When thinking about your spending in retirement, what matters most are your sources of income. These typically include your Social Security income; potentially, income from a pension plan; and the income generated from your investment portfolio (both retirement and personal investment assets).

As a general guideline, when we look at the income from your investment portfolio, we figure that you can, at the outset of retirement, safely withdraw about 4 to 5% from your portfolio on an annual basis to cover expenses in retirement and still expect to maintain your financial independence over the long term. That means if you have $1 million saved when you retire, you can safely take out $40,000 to $50,000 per year; if you have $2 million, you'll be able to withdraw $80,000 to $100,000. The withdrawal amount can increase as you get older, as we'll discuss later.

Understanding and planning for your income and spending needs is critical to making smart investment decisions. We illustrate this using a funnel approach, shown in Figure 1.1: Funnel #1, your Income Funnel, is for your steady income, which includes Social Security, pension, any annuitized income, and salary if you are still working, either full or part time; Funnel #2, your Portfolio Funnel, is for your assets. The income from Funnel #1 should be your first source of funds for living expenses. If you have excess income flowing through Funnel #1 – meaning that you are spending less than your primary income sources bring in – then the excess goes into Funnel #2 and adds to your investment portfolio.

Having excess money to pour into Funnel #2 is a terrific scenario, but unless you are still working or have a significant pension income, that happens only rarely. More often, our clients are spending more than their primary sources of income bring in, so they need to get income from their investment portfolio. Here, Funnel #2 comes into play: We need to allocate your assets so that they provide a 4 to 5% annual distribution that – when combined with the income from Funnel #1 – is a comfortable amount for you to live on. This is the key to a financially successful retirement.

Being too conservative and allocating all your assets to short-term bonds or low-risk investments means that you may not be able to withdraw what you need in retirement. Investing too aggressively can result in losses that may completely disrupt your assets, which means you may not be able to withdraw at a rate that can support you in retirement. Getting Funnel #2 invested correctly is critical to bringing you peace of mind and achieving your long-term retirement goals.

Building Your Portfolio

You should build your portfolio around two main factors: (1) How much risk you can *afford* to take and (2) how much risk you are *willing* to take. The amount of risk you can afford to take is the critical decision, and this depends on how much you spend now and how much you expect to spend in the future.

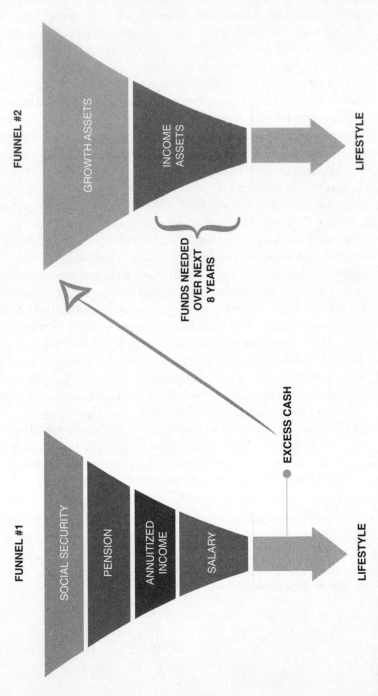

FUNNEL #2

GROWTH ASSETS

INCOME ASSETS

LIFESTYLE

FUNDS NEEDED OVER NEXT 8 YEARS

EXCESS CASH

FUNNEL #1

SOCIAL SECURITY

PENSION

ANNUITIZED INCOME

SALARY

LIFESTYLE

Figure 1.1   The Retirement Funnels

10

The risk you are willing to take depends on your personal tolerance, which was likely shaped in your childhood by your family. It is interesting to me that a client's level of education does not seem to have any bearing on his or her risk tolerance. Being well educated, with an advanced degree such as an MD or JD, or even an MBA, does not mean that a person will have any better understanding of investment risk (and therefore greater risk tolerance) than someone with only a high school education.

My dad never completed college, but he had a great understanding of investment risk. He was a terrific investor because he grew up in a family that was active and somewhat daring with their investments, and he was a great student of investing, reading all the investment classics. I still have his copy of Benjamin Graham's *Security Analysis,* and many others from his library, on my bookshelf.

Mom grew up on a hog farm in Illinois and married my dad when she was eighteen, two weeks after they met on a blind date. She didn't study investing like my father did, but she has a keen understanding of her cash flow and of the risk she can and is willing to take. Understanding this stuff doesn't require a PhD or a degree in finance, but it does help to have someone with knowledge and experience to guide you. Most people would be surprised to see that, at age 86, my mom is mainly invested in stocks, mostly dividend paying, rather than bonds. Sure, I get the call from her when the markets are not being kind to us investors, but her question isn't as much about the loss in market value as it is about making sure her income is secure and her dividends are still going to be paid.

Build your portfolio around your forecasted cash needs, investing the amount you are likely to need over an eight-year period in lower-risk assets. Let's assume you retire at age 66 and you can start collecting Social Security and/or pension income at that time. For the purposes of our example, let's say you will collect $40,000 in Social Security and pension income, and that you do not have any salary or other source of income outside your portfolio income. Next, let's assume your annual cash flow needs are $120,000 per year.

Begin by making sure you have a secure source of investment assets to support that additional income need of $80,000 ($120,000 – $40,000). There are two ways to do this, and the method you choose will depend on the size of your portfolio. If you have a portfolio large enough, one in which the interest and dividends are equal to or greater than the $80,000 income need, then you can build an income-based portfolio of bonds and dividend-paying stocks. Otherwise, you will need to rely on interest, dividends, and long-term growth.

Given a portfolio of $2 million, we would allocate $640,000 ($80,000 × 8) in lower-risk income-producing assets (certificates of deposit [CDs] and bonds) and the remaining $1,360,000 ($2 million – $640,000) in longer-term growth assets (stocks, real estate, and alternative assets). This puts 68% of your assets in a long-term growth position and 32% in lower-risk income-producing assets. Think of the $640,000 as your umbrella – you want it available when it rains!

Why do we multiply your annual income need by eight? That is a good question. We have found over the years that stock market volatility is one of the biggest concerns for our clients, and it can create one of the largest disruptions to a client's portfolio if not handled properly. Stock market cycles (the up and down volatility) vary greatly but are typically not more than five or six years in length. If you must sell your investments during a down cycle, it can be very difficult to recover from losses and maintain your lifestyle. So we create an umbrella that protects you from those rainy days. We build your portfolio with eight years of safe assets that won't be as volatile during a downturn. You can use those assets to meet your cash flow needs, which allows the more volatile assets eight years to move through the cycle and recover.

To consider yourself financially independent, you need to have enough secure assets to get you through any market cycle. If the market takes a big tumble, you don't want that drop to upset your retirement plans. History shows us that a decline in the markets will occur, often when we are not expecting it. That is why you need the umbrella – you don't want to be forced to sell quality long-term assets at the wrong time. The success of your investment strategy will depend on your discipline in staying with your investment allocation when the markets get rocky.

In my 30-plus years as a financial planner, I have never seen a situation in which a client followed the process we outlined and then ran short because the portfolio didn't perform properly. When clients have accumulated enough in retirement savings during their working years and yet later struggled to maintain their financial independence, it is typically because they've made decisions based on emotion and spent assets in a way that isn't aligned with their plan.

As you age, the percentage you can withdraw from your portfolio per year may rise because your time horizon is not as lengthy – the span of time you will need your money to last is shorter. This will depend, of course, on the level of assets you started with. But when you are in your 80s, it may be perfectly reasonable to relax the spending guidelines. A general rule of thumb is to spend 4 to 5% of your portfolio each year in your 60s, 5 to 6% in your 70s, 6 to 7% in your 80s, and 7 to 8% in your 90s. Expect longevity. Once you have reached age 80, your life expectancy is nearly 89 years (88.20 for men and 89.64 for women in the United States), according to the Social Security Administration's actuarial life table.[5] Remember, these are averages, so 50% of people live beyond these life expectancies.

Ironically, it is at just about the 80-year mark that people typically begin to slow their spending. It is the rare 80-something who is contemplating going on an African safari. Most people in that age range are less able to travel or are less interested in it; they tend to go out less frequently to restaurants or the theater; and they are more likely to be giving away their material possessions than looking to acquire new ones. In these years, spending tends to naturally decline unless a big health-care expense arises, at which point it can pick up again.

We also see that in down years people tend naturally to spend less. When markets dip 10, 15, or 20%, behavior changes automatically. Most people will say, let's postpone that lavish trip to Europe or let's not buy the new car this year. I have watched this happen all across the income and wealth spectrum, even with wealthy clients who have $20 or $30 million. A single vacation or a new car, no matter how extravagant, would not affect the portfolios of these clients in any meaningful way, but they will tighten their belts, so to speak, until the markets recover. There's a basic human impulse to conserve in lean times, and the majority of people follow it. But I use the word *majority* for good reason.

Getting Carried Away by Your Passions

Overspending would not be a retirement fail if every person were able to rein in spending and follow the guidelines we've discussed. Unfortunately, some people cannot, and in these cases compulsive spending poses a serious threat in the retirement period, when income is typically curtailed. Ranging from too-frequent "splurges" to a pattern of compulsive spending that gets progressively worse over time, a shopping habit can take many forms.

On a daily basis we're assailed by approximately 3,000 advertisements, according to some sources, and these marketing messages are designed to convince us that we *need* the product or service on offer, and further that we *deserve* it.[6] With modern marketing telling us that we are what we buy and assuring us that the lavish lifestyles we see depicted in popular media are within our reach – and with easy credit all too available – it's not surprising that many of us get in over our heads.

Some people cannot seem to stop spending in areas about which they are passionate – and if the passion is an expensive one, it is easy for spending to spiral out of control. Collecting sports cars, boating, and horse racing are big-ticket leisure activities that come to mind. If a client has a passion for horses and racing and has the wherewithal to indulge initially, it can be easy to justify ongoing expenditures. When a racehorse that has had some success is injured just before an imagined big payoff, it's tempting to invest in another. And another. The payoff is always just out of reach, but the person has perpetual hope that the next horse is going to be a fantastic thing.

The problem is compounded when the outlay is not a one-time investment (and it rarely is); in our horse racing example, there are costs for trainers, grooms, exercise riders, blacksmith, veterinarian, and jockey; for supplies like bandages, feed, and bedding; and for stable and race entry fees and so on. Most high-stakes hobbies are similar – the associated costs are ongoing, and the more deeply involved you are, the higher the costs can go.

When the hobby that absorbs so much of your money is also the hub around which your social activity revolves, it's easy to get sucked in deeper, and the cycle is reinforced. Sometimes the spending is subtly (or not so subtly) about competition – when your friends and acquaintances are high rollers, you naturally want to keep up with them.

One way to stay involved with your passion but limit your financial obligation is to scale back your commitment without abandoning your hobby entirely. Our client with a passion for horse racing opted to buy a small share in a thoroughbred rather than taking on the entire ownership obligation. That way, he maintained a stake and was able to participate, but he wasn't on the hook for runaway costs.

Depending on the activity, there are multiple options for continuing to enjoy your hobby without spending a fortune: Partnering with others, renting rather than buying, or reducing the time you spend on your hobby can all help keep your plan in balance.

Habitual Overspending

There is a category of overspenders who are less likely to have a consuming passion and more likely to just consistently spend more than they need to or can afford to. While any one expense – shoes, jewelry, furniture, concerts, meals at fine restaurants, vacations – may be reasonable, the pattern of spending can be a concern over time. Some people seem to have "overspending" as a personality trait, and they don't worry about large outflows of cash. Indeed, as long as the inflow is well above the outflow – even if the spending is what most of us would consider excessive – it may not be a problem. But when income drops and spending can't be controlled, difficulties arise quickly.

Experts describe a range of behaviors and attitudes with regard to money, from the healthy spender to the problem spender to the addictive spender. The act of buying can become a security blanket – people use it to calm themselves and make themselves feel good. For these spenders, shopping can boost their mood or relieve feelings of boredom or anxiety.

Indulging themselves (or others) gives such spenders a short-lived burst of self-worth, and they may overspend on services as well as on material goods. Often, husbands overspend on their wives and kids, and women on their husbands, children, and friends – these types of gifts feel acceptable because they demonstrate love for family and friends, and that sort of gift giving has the stamp of social approval. Indeed, there is nothing wrong with being generous toward your loved ones. The key indicator of healthy spending behavior is that the price of the item falls easily within your set budget without edging out other priorities.

According to a survey conducted by *Money* magazine, 22% of husbands and wives have spent money they didn't want their spouse to find out about. For women, the stealth items were clothing, shoes, and gifts for family and friends; for men, the clandestine purchases were for hobbies and electronics.[7]

There are times when the conversations about spending patterns are made more difficult by a complicated dynamic between husband and wife. In one particular case, married clients had stark differences in spending, financial interest, and age. Fred is married – a second marriage – to a woman who is about a dozen years younger than he is. While Fred brought most of the assets to the marriage and is very knowledgeable about their portfolio, his wife, Sharon, is not interested in financial matters. Sharon, however, has a spending habit that will eventually create a major problem for them, despite the fact that they had retired with a sizable nest egg. Our analysis shows that in the next 12 to 14 years this couple will need to downsize their home dramatically and lower their standard of living. The problem, ironically, will probably be Sharon's ultimately, as she is statistically likely to outlive her older husband.

Though we had several conversations with Fred – who attended our advisory sessions alone – about outsized household spending, Sharon's spending continued and he clearly felt unable to influence her behavior. Eventually, he gave up. The outcome for Fred and Sharon is still uncertain, as both continue to be healthy, but they have not curbed their spending in any meaningful way and their situation is not sustainable indefinitely. If they don't find a more balanced path, one or both – should they both live well into old age – may find that they've run out of money.

The scenario can be alarming for a surviving spouse, who may not realize how dramatically benefits will drop when the spouse dies. When a spouse passes away, Social Security payments can go down by a third and the pension for the surviving spouse may be cut by half or two-thirds, or may go away completely. If the surviving spouse has not been engaged in the discussions about finances, the reduced income may come as a shock.

When Generosity Goes Awry

Though it may seem counterintuitive, charitable giving can also represent a problematic form of overspending, and can be particularly difficult to address because it comes out of the best of our human impulses – the desire to do good in the world and to share our wealth with those who are less fortunate. Making a large gift to a worthy cause – to fund cancer research, to supply medical aid in a war-torn country, or to endow cultural institutions – feels good and brings accolades from the organization and your peers.

But some people feel compelled to give even when their portfolio is shrinking significantly. In these cases, making major donations on an annual basis impacts your investment accounts in a way that will ultimately leave you vulnerable. And unlike some other forms of spending, say on a vacation home that could be sold, the outlay can never be recovered.

We have a client who was committed to several charities that he had been involved in over the years, and he was widely known and respected for his work with them. He felt compelled to continue to give each year at the same level that he had in previous years, when he was actively working. His income had declined significantly, however, and his generous gifts meant that withdrawals from the couple's portfolio exceeded our preferred withdrawal range.

Although the couple was well aware of the dangers inherent in giving at the high level they had set before they retired, they continued, jeopardizing their lifestyle and ultimately putting a strain on their personal health. Slowing their contributions was obviously in their best interest, yet they were unwilling, or perhaps felt unable, to make the adjustment. That spending simply made them feel good and helped maintain their identity.

I have learned not to underestimate the importance of maintaining one's identity in retirement. As you transition from your years of active work and child-rearing to a period in which your activities are more self-directed, it can be easy to lose your sense of self. Some people seek to preserve their sense of identity by holding on to the activities or patterns that defined their lives before they retired. As we'll see throughout the book, avoiding retirement fail depends in part on navigating a smooth transition in which you find new ways to add purpose and fulfillment to your life.

Reining In Spending

One of the best ways to curb unnecessary spending is to assess what *necessary* spending is. Sit down, with your partner if you have one, and decide what your spending will be for the upcoming month – *then stick to it*. Include all your essentials and leave a cushion for unexpected expenses and a couple of treats, but remember that the exercise is about taking control of your spending and prioritizing in line with your ultimate goals. While *budget* feels like an outdated word, tracking your expenses and staying aware of where discretionary spending is running amok can help you make sound decisions about what you really should be laying out for which items or experiences.

Overspenders who have gotten into a deep hole will likely not be able to fix their problems by simply cutting out the morning latte or putting the designer suit back on the rack, however. More drastic action, such as selling a home that is realistically outside your budget or forgoing expensive family trips, should be on the table. Look with clear eyes at your overall picture and make the hard choices.

For a few, spending is an outright addiction not unlike alcoholism or drug addiction. Just as some people go into a bar and have to drink, and drink hard, some people have to shop hard. Chronic overspending that gets progressively worse can seriously jeopardize a person's retirement, as he or she spends down assets at a rate that is not sustainable. Those with truly disordered spending may have underlying emotional or psychological reasons for their behavior, and people who cannot gain control despite an awareness of the situation should consider counseling with a therapist who specializes in the treatment of financial disorders.

Fortunately, most overspenders are not so extreme. As we saw with Julia at the opening of the chapter, many people simply become used to a certain lifestyle and continue to spend freely, even when their income and asset levels can't sustain such outlays. Knowing how much money you have coming in, where your money goes, and what your projections for retirement are helps you make financial decisions that will put you on firm ground as you head into your post-work life.

Help for Overspenders

- Develop a good financial plan that outlines your goals, estimates your expenses accurately, offers clarity about what you can safely spend, and provides for emergencies. Working with an advisor can help you get good, objective advice about what you can afford to spend and how to invest the balance wisely.

- Downsize if you must. Often, tinkering around the margins will not help your overall financial picture if your assets have dissipated past a certain point. It may be time to move to a smaller house and adopt a lifestyle that fits your budget well.

- Continue working longer. The converse of the prescription to cut spending is, of course, to bring in more income. Working longer, or returning to work if you've retired already, provides additional income to offset your spending needs and can help you build up your retirement assets again; and when you retire later, you will not need as much savings for that period.

- Consider other ways to enjoy your passions. As Jim Bruyette, my partner at SBSB, says, "Don't buy the boat. Make a friend who has a boat." Judge which expenses will truly bring you and your family lasting pleasure and which may be passing fancies. There are often other ways to enjoy the things you want to do, such as renting or sharing – or making friends.

- Seek professional help if your spending is truly out of control. If you can't seem to stick to a reasonable spending plan despite your best efforts, consider consulting a therapist who specializes in disordered financial behavior.

CHAPTER 2

The Nest That Won't Empty

Lauren, a longtime client, called me in something of a panic one morning, saying she and her husband, John, had gotten an emergency call from their son asking for help. Jeffrey and his wife had tuition coming due for their two children (Lauren's grandchildren), who were attending private colleges, and they needed money to pay the bills. As you can imagine, Lauren was anxious to help because she knows how important education is to her grandchildren's future success. Unfortunately, though, this is not the first time we have received this sort of call from Lauren.

What is interesting about this story is that Lauren and John's son is a highly successful attorney in his early fifties who lives in a beautiful home, enjoys traveling, loves spending time at the couple's second home on the lake, and has been exceedingly generous to the church the family attends. Over the years, mom and dad have always been there to help out when finances got tight for Jeffrey. As usual, my client asks, "Greg, can you help make this happen in the next couple of weeks? The tuition is due by the end of July." I answer, "Yes, Lauren, of course we can make it happen." But then I suggest gently that we make it a loan, so Jeffrey has an obligation to pay the money back. And the normal response we receive is, "A loan isn't necessary. Of course they will pay it back, once they get the children out of college."

I explained that, if Lauren and John passed away before the money was paid back, the other children would receive less in their inheritance because of the many gifts to Jeffrey and his family. "Is that what you intend?" I asked them. They understood my concern on this point, and had told me before that they wanted to be fair and to treat all their children equally. Though it felt at first as if they weren't being generous when their son needed them, the loan idea ultimately made sense to them.

Aging Fledglings

When I talk about the nest that won't empty, I'm not talking about kids who literally will not leave home – though, to be sure, that can also be a challenge for some parents. What I'm talking about here are situations where the kids continue to be a drain on their parents' finances well after they should be flying on their own. We see this over and over again: Grown children, some of them in their 40s or 50s and with advanced degrees, are taking money from their parents at a rate those parents can ill afford.

The fact is that simply having children has a negative impact on a person's wealth accumulation – those little bundles of joy represent a bundle of cash, not only in terms of expenses (to feed, clothe, entertain, and educate) but also in lost income – one or both parents must often curtail their own income-producing activities to care for the children, at least temporarily, resulting in reduced opportunity to build their assets. According to a recent report, a middle-income couple raising two children can expect to pay $233,610 for a child born in 2015.[1] And that is only through age 17 – so college expenses are not included!

But, of course, we don't – and we shouldn't – look at our children with a jaundiced eye, thinking about how much they will cost us. We love them and support them, and want them to be happy. That's what good parents do. The question is really how long do we support them, and at what level? What are the consequences of excessive support, both for us and for them?

A study conducted by the Pew Research Center in 2013 showed that 73% of adults in their 40s and 50s had provided financial support to a grown child in the prior year, and more than half of those parents reported being that child's primary means of support.[2] Some of the kids were in school, but more than a third were not. The financial crisis of 2008–2009 and the recession, together with the sluggish recovery that followed, are at least partly to blame for the phenomenon of young people requiring more support from their parents, but a cultural shift has taken place, too. Many parents, particularly affluent parents, have unwittingly created a sense of entitlement in their children. The kids have always been on the receiving end of their parents' largesse, and they don't understand why that should stop.

A TD Bank study found that women were more likely than men to say that they are the one who spoils the kids with money – 42% of women compared with 28% of men.[3]

There are four main reasons that adult children put a strain on their parents' finances. Some of these situations are unavoidable or temporary, while others are much more controllable, at least in theory. We'll talk about each of these factors and later discuss some issues to be aware of as well as ways to address the matter. These four categories are ongoing support needed because of a child's illness or disability; an excessive focus on education, especially private schooling and elite colleges; a change in life circumstances for a child; and good old-fashioned failure of kids to fully grow up. Each of these situations has a different impact on your assets and retirement plans, and each necessitates a different way of thinking about preparation and solutions.

Life's Roulette Wheel

It's the spin of the wheel: A child is born with or develops a physical, mental, or emotional need, or perhaps suffers an accident, that requires that he be supported by his parents to a greater degree than most children would need. The support necessary will vary widely, of course, depending upon the particular situation. Some children will require their parents' continued financial assistance, to varying degrees, throughout their adulthood, and indeed may rely on support from parents even after those parents have passed away.

Continuing support for an adult child with special needs is something that parents must plan for, and your financial planner can help you explore options for securing your child's future, both during your retirement and beyond. Sitting down with a financial professional to develop a strong financial plan that accounts for the help you can give, together with any other sources of income the child may have, is a good first step.

A trust is one tool that we recommend to parents who are looking to ensure their child's future financial well-being; a trust can be established during your lifetime and can operate in tandem with your will, allowing any inheritance you leave your child to pass into the trust. Depending upon your assets and the needs of your child, you may wish to set up a special needs trust, which is designed to supplement government or private assistance. Make sure to include both your financial planner and an estate lawyer in your decisions, so that the plan is well constructed and financially optimal. It's important to look at what you can really contribute and plan around the realities of that number. (We'll talk more about trusts in Chapter 8, "Life's Unpredictabilities.")

The Harvard or Bust Syndrome

We've been conditioned to believe that education is critically important – and it is. Over the course of their careers, college graduates earn an average of 66% more than those with a high school diploma, and they are also far less likely to face unemployment.[4] When you look at earnings over a lifetime, those workers with a bachelor's degree earn approximately $1 million more than those without.

But it's also possible to overfund education, sometimes to the detriment of both your retirement account and your kids' happiness. As my colleague Gary Ingram tells his clients, "There's no scholarship for retirement." Your kids can get grants, loans, and/or scholarships that will help them cover the cost of their education, but there's no way you can generate need-based or scholarship-based income in retirement. Your kids also have a lot of earning years to pay off any debt they may incur in paying for college, but you will have a limited number of years to make up for the dent in your retirement savings that can come as a result of footing hefty bills for your kids' schooling.

Helping your kids pay for their higher education is an admirable goal and can be a worthwhile investment. Depending on your circumstances, you may be well positioned to provide a lot of assistance. But as you and your kids are considering colleges, be realistic about the size of the contribution you can wisely make and be careful not to underwrite a massive tuition bill to the detriment of your retirement savings. Your financial advisor will be able to work with you to develop a plan to help you determine the impact of proposed education spending on your overall financial independence.

There's no right or wrong answer – what's important is that you clearly understand the impact and trade-offs of your desires.

Tax-advantaged education plans, such as 529 plans (so named because they are authorized under Section 529 of the Internal Revenue Code), are tremendous vehicles that allow you to save in a thoughtful way for your children's college expenses—and, as of 2018, for K-12 private school, too. If you can afford to fund a 529 plan, we suggest aiming to put 90% of the expected cost of college education into the account. For example, if you project that your child's higher education costs will be $25,000 per year ($100,000 for four years), try to invest, over time, $90,000 into the plan.

Hopefully, the 529 plan assets will grow at the same rate as, or even more than, the rate at which college tuition increases. Review the account annually to see if you need to make any adjustments.

Why fund the plan at only 90%? Our recommendation is to make sure you don't overfund your 529 plan because there are unpleasant tax consequences if you take the money out and don't use it for post–secondary education. The 90% provides a buffer if the investments in the 529 accounts have great performance and grow larger than the amount you need for college costs; or you may not need the entire account if your child gets a scholarship or doesn't complete all four years of schooling.

And if your kids are still young, you might take a hard look at whether that elite nursery school, the thirteen years of private K–12 schooling, and an expensive college to follow, is really what is best – for you *and* your child. Sometimes parents get so caught up in the idea that, to succeed, their kids must have a beginning-to-end elite education that they fail to recognize that their child may not thrive in that kind of competitive environment. The good news, if your child does attend K-12 private school, is that the Tax Cuts and Jobs Act of 2017 allows you to use up to $10,000 per year from a child's 529 plan for tuition. Most states provide a tax incentive to invest in 529 plans, so in addition to the tax-free compounding in the account, you may save on state income taxes.

Our clients Isaac and Lillian really hoped that their son, Jason, would attend a certain Ivy League university. They were driven by the idea that this particular university was where their child needed to be, and no other school would do. I tried coaching them through the process, asking if they knew what their son was interested in and where he wanted to go to school, but they felt certain he wasn't in a position to understand the importance of the acclaimed private college he could attend.

Where does Jason end up going to college? To his parents' Ivy League school of choice. Unfortunately, the university wasn't a good fit for him, and he ended up miserable and doing poorly in his classes. After a few semesters, his parents begrudgingly brought him home. Because Jason was unhappy living at home, his doting (and now worried) mom and dad set him up in an apartment. He didn't have money of his own, so they were supporting him while he tried to figure out what to do.

While Jason's parents love him dearly and have only his best interests at heart, it is all too easy for their intensive support to become more or less permanent – this is a pattern we see repeated, and it is not a pattern that is ultimately healthy for either parents or kids. Your children will certainly benefit from your attention and guidance when they are researching schools, career options, relocation possibilities, and other major life decisions, but in the end they need to find their own way.

Let's not leave Jason on that bleak note, though. I am pleased to say that he did eventually return to college, to a non–Ivy League school – and although it took a few semesters for him to gain his footing, he found a school that was great for him. He graduated and is now out blazing a trail in the business world. I wonder what guidance he will give his children when they are ready to go off to college?

A Rocky Path

Adult children may be out of the house and doing well when circumstances intervene to make them need your help again. A child may lose his job and require temporary support. Or a married child may divorce, wreaking havoc on her finances. Especially when the adult child is a stay-at-home parent without a great deal of work experience or with many responsibilities at home, the parents of the adult child may need or want to step in and provide support. This feels particularly urgent when grandchildren are in the picture.

Such support can be a slippery slope, though, with the adult child gradually becoming dependent on the money. The amount of help you can offer will depend on the child's particular situation and on your own financial wherewithal. A get-in, get-out kind of aid is usually not a problem – everybody needs help once in a while, and most people's savings can take a few hits – but too often, short-term assistance turns into a lifetime, or near-lifetime, of support.

When we see a couple with an adult child who experiences a setback, we try to help them navigate the kind of aid they can safely give. Del and Louise, for example, have a daughter who has a child with autism. Because of the child's needs, their daughter, Rachel, couldn't work, and the family was struggling. Del and Louise were helping financially, but Louise had been a stay-at-home mom, and the couple's retirement account was not going to be able to sustain the kind of contributions they were making on a long-term basis.

After analysis of the situation, and a lot of discussion, we finally got to a solution. Del and Louise sold their house and downsized to a smaller house very near their daughter's. Selling your home may seem like a drastic step, but it was a way for them to achieve a majority of the goals on their list. They could better afford to help their daughter's family financially without jeopardizing their own future, and both Del and Louise could also provide more emotional support and child care. As Louise stepped in to do more daily care, Rachel was able to go back to work, which put her family in a better financial position as well.

Laying out a realistic financial picture, and then talking through priorities and being creative with solutions, can yield great results, as it did for this family. In other cases, however, the financial situation is more dire or the parties are less able to compromise.

Failure to Launch

Kids who don't learn to truly fly on their own represent perhaps the largest category, certainly in the sense that the phenomenon affects a great number of our clients as well as people around the country. The good news is that, unlike an unexpected event or a difficult circumstance, this is an area over which you, as a parent, have a great deal of control. But you need to seize that control. It's easiest to start when kids are young, making sure they know that you expect they will grow up and become self-sufficient. But for many people who are nearing retirement age or are already into their post-work years, it is already too late to establish early the importance of their children's financial independence.

When we see families that are leaking money, we need to have a difficult conversation. Typically, one or both of the parents will tell me, "It's so much harder for our children these days. Look how expensive homes are now, look how expensive cars are – how can little Johnny [now age 35, I might add], afford these things without our help?" The story won't leave their heads that their children really need them. If I'm not there to help, they believe, my kids won't be able to have the kind of life I've had. And, of course, they're your kids! You love them and want them to be happy.

It can be difficult for us to let our older kids, college-age or even older, make decisions without our input. I have been there myself. My daughter, Lisa, quit her job and bought a one-way ticket to Southeast Asia. She said, "I am burned out from work and need a break, so I'm going to go to Thailand." I didn't try to persuade her to stay here or to get another job. I didn't do anything but wish her safe travels and ask her what she was doing for Christmas.

When I tell this story, some people are appalled that I would let my daughter, who was 25 at the time, go to Thailand by herself. But she was an adult, though young, and she could make her own choices. Sure, I sometimes worried about her and felt a bit anxious when I didn't hear from her for a few weeks. But this was her adventure, not mine, and it ended up being a great experience for her. She traveled the country, enjoyed learning about a culture very different from the one she'd grown up in, met many wonderful people who were on similar adventures, and really learned to rely on her own resources. Eventually, she came back home, ready to get back to work. She is now settled in the Grand Caymans, teaching accounting and economics. It is a wonderful life she lives!

The best thing I could do for Lisa was to let her go and find her own way. She is smart and talented, and I knew she would figure it out. But I didn't give her any money. Friends say, "How can she afford to do that?" I tell them, "That's her issue. If she can't afford it, she'll come home and get another job." But she did fine. And that is my point when I share this story. My daughter did fine. And your kids will do fine without your help, too.

Sometimes, parents are wedded to the idea that they are so important in their children's lives that the kids can't get along without them. They want to stay relevant. But there are better ways to be relevant in your children's lives than to encourage them to depend on you.

A colleague of mine here at SBSB, Barbara Schelhorn, notes that when people have problems saying no to their adult children's requests for money, it's usually because the parents are people pleasers with a strong desire to make their children happy. "They want their children to love them and to view them as a good mother or a good father," Barbara says. "Every parent wants that, of course, but when that desire is too strong, when the relationship is out of balance, there are going to be problems."

At this point, there are two separate questions: (1) Does the money you are giving jeopardize your own financial health and future? and (2) Does doling out cash really help your child? If a child has a health problem or a setback of some other kind, that's one thing, but often the child's dependence is based on a dynamic between the parent and child.

If the amount of money you're gifting is small enough (or if you are wealthy enough) that it has no significant negative impact on your finances, then your continued support may be fine. But for many people, that will not be the case: The amounts are large and/or the impact is significant. Even if you are able to afford the cash, you still need to answer the second question: Are you really helping your child when you allow her to remain dependent?

Am I Jeopardizing My Own Future?

Entry into the adult world can be tough, and many parents try to soften the blow for their children. They don't want to think of their kids sitting in a tiny apartment eating instant ramen (even though that's what they did), so they pony up until the kids can get on their feet. The problem comes when kids don't pull things together quickly, or at all, or when parents' contributions threaten to undermine their own financial security. Most couples nearing traditional retirement age need to continue to work, and they are having to work longer, only because they spend so much money trying to keep their children going.

More young adults are living with their parents than at any time since 1880. Among 18- to 34-year-olds, just over 32% are living with their parents.[5]

Even more problematic are some older kids – even into their 40s, 50s, or 60s – who continue to depend on their parents. In some instances, the children may simply not realize the toll they are taking on their parents' finances. They figure their parents have enough money to go around, and they never stop to consider that their parents may outlive their wealth. Parents who've always provided for their children may be unwilling or unable to say no.

When you are making decisions about whether to come to your kids' financial rescue, it's helpful to think through all the outcomes of your decision, specifically the things that you *don't* want to have happen. For example, you may never want to be dependent on your children or to have your children need to change their own plans so they can care for you later in life. Once you are clear about the worst-case scenarios you want to avoid, you can make sure you are heading toward an outcome that you *do* want. And if laying out large amounts of cash to help your children reach their immediate goals will jeopardize your long-range plans, then you may be undermining their future happiness as well as yours.

We all, no matter our financial circumstance, have to assess what we have and prioritize our goals. Start with the numbers: Think through what you have and what you want, and build around that. Have an honest conversation with your financial advisor, who is experienced in projecting the costs of the things you want to do and can help you understand the trade-offs you might need to make to enforce your priorities.

Everybody should be evaluating the impact of their spending, no matter their income level or wealth. List all your priorities: I want to remain financially independent; I want to take one nice vacation a year; I want to be able to help my child with her rent if she needs it. And if you can't afford to do all the things you want, which ones are the most important? When it comes down to it, helping family tends to take priority over lots of other things.

In most cases, parents and kids ultimately want the same thing and they just have to agree on how to get there. Ruth had been giving her daughter Heidi sums of money whenever her daughter expressed a need or a desire. Ruth was essentially handing a blank check over to her child with alarming regularity. But when I spoke to Heidi, with Ruth's permission, of course, they were able to get on the same page.

I asked Heidi if she would like her mom to move in with her when Ruth's assets were depleted and she would be forced to sell her home.

That put a new spin on the discussion. Heidi was truly unaware that her mom's financial well-being was endangered by the money she was giving so freely. Since Ruth's husband had passed away, her income was greatly reduced because she was receiving only a fraction of the Social Security and pension income they'd been getting as a couple. Ruth would be fine – as long as she didn't give all her assets away.

We all wanted the same thing: For Ruth to be happy and to do well and to not end up living with Heidi. We were able to agree on a small amount that Ruth could afford to give each year, given her financial picture, and that worked out very well.

I've also had scenarios that did not end as well, mainly because occasionally a child believes that his priorities are most important. If you have a child who is adamant and a parent who gives in, particularly if that parent is widowed and there is no other source of moral support when it comes to these tough decisions, then the parent may well choose to drain assets attempting to placate the child.

One strategy we have used for scenarios in which kids are coming and asking for money on an as-needed (or wanted) basis is to create a trust account for the kids; the parents are then able to tell the children, "This is all you get. The trust will distribute a set amount each year, but you can't come back and ask for more." In one recent instance, this strategy did not prevent a child from coming back and asking; but our clients were able to say, no, we all agreed on this amount, and that is all that can be given at this time.

We've also written loans from the parent to a child, and formalized the arrangement that way. A loan instrument in black and white, outlining the expectation of repayment – including invoices that are sent like bills – can be a powerful motivator, preventing the child from asking irresponsibly for more money. And if the child should fail to repay, the loan is part of the estate, which can lessen tensions with other siblings. Trust me, the other kids in the family are generally not happy when one sibling is asking for and receiving large amounts of cash from mom and dad. A loan agreement can reduce the financial impact on the other children and take away some of the animosity that may result when parents gift a substantial amount of money to a child.

These approaches can provide structure and accountability, forestalling a slide down the slippery slope to a retirement account that has been hollowed out, perhaps unwittingly, by grown kids. Even if not all goes precisely according to plan, the structure creates a sense of deliberateness; it's much easier to view and raise red flags if outflows are documented as loans or regulated by a trust or other agreement.

Am I Really Helping My Kids?

Even if you had all the money in the world, I wouldn't counsel you to hand it over unquestioningly to your child. The value of money and hard work, as well as responsibility in terms of finances, are learned. Kids don't hit age 18 and magically think, hey, I should get a job and start paying my own way. Most kids, even those who seem to take and take from their parents, aren't selfish or greedy. Their parents have created the situation by providing for their children, sometimes extravagantly, while failing to show them what it takes to be able to afford those things or allowing them to experiment with their own finances.

Often, "entitlement" is a phenomenon that characterizes every other generation. One generation is self-made and becomes very successful because of the values they hold around hard work and sacrifice and self-reliance, but then they want to give their kids what they didn't have. There are a lot of 50- and 60-year-olds who are children of blue-collar parents, but they've done well and now they want to educate their kids in private schools and make sure the kids have all the creature comforts and luxuries that their friends have.

We call it entitlement, but it's just that these parents haven't instilled in their kids the values that they grew up with. The children are not necessarily spoiled, but they don't understand the hard work or education it takes to make an income that allows people to live at the level their parents enjoy and share with them.

The kids get out of college and expect that they will have the same lifestyle they had while living at home, but they haven't built their own financial base. Parents look at the kids and say, "Well, my child can't make the mortgage payment, my child can't pay my grandson's tuition, I have to pay it for him," rather than helping him retrench and learn to live on what he brings in.

If your kids are young, let them make some of their own financial decisions and mistakes. Don't protect them from the consequences of their poor decisions – for example, don't step in and pay for something they want just because they've blown through their allowance. Don't rush to help them solve money problems or be the white knight who gives them everything they want so they never learn to save. This can be hard, I know. It's especially difficult if you live in an affluent area where other parents are showering their kids with the latest high-end electronics and even with expensive cars.

My kids grew up hearing stories of my childhood days. I grew up in Pittsburgh and attended the public high school in my neighborhood. My parents were determined that all four of their children would go to college – and they succeeded with that goal. They couldn't afford to buy us cars or send us to private school. The four of us kids worked during our college years to pay for books and for our spending money, and all was good. That seemed pretty normal to me.

Fast-forward twenty years, and I am living in a nice neighborhood in McLean, Virginia. As my son, David, neared age 16 and his friends were starting to drive, many of his friends' parents were buying their kids cars. Nothing wrong with that. Having an extra driver in the house is a huge help for many families. However, when I was growing up, my parents didn't buy me a car and I'd always told my own children, "I will provide you with the things you need – food, clothing, shelter, books, education, and so on. But I don't buy cars."

When David turned 16, he got his driver's license immediately. We let him know he could drive the family station wagon when it was available. One day he came to me and said, "So Dad, let's go look at cars." And I said, "Cool, let's do it."

As we buckled ourselves into our seats, I asked him, "How much money do you have?" And he said, "What?" I said, "How much money do you have to buy this car? They're not going to just give it to you." His face fell, and he said, "Well, Dad, I thought you could help me out." I told him, "Okay, I can probably make you a loan of 50% of the purchase price, and typical loan terms require a three-year payback." We got back out of the car.

It was a quick lesson in the kind of principles I wanted to impart to my child. I want him to value self-reliance and to understand that it's important to live within your means, whatever those means may be. So he got to drive the station wagon, when it was available. Ultimately, David turned the situation to his advantage. He named the station wagon "Big Sexy," and I would hear him talking with his friends about going somewhere and he would say, "Let me check with my folks and see if we can take Big Sexy."

This is a story I share because I know how hard it can be to say no to your kids. I've been there, too, and I know what it's like. We want to please our sons and daughters. We want to be their friends and for them to like us. By saying no we jeopardize that relationship, or so we think.

I'm not saying that you need to make the same decision about a car or any other specific item, but it's important to set that boundary with your child when he's still a child. Have open conversations with your children, when they are young, and set their expectations. Amazingly, if you ask my son about that experience today, at age 30, he will tell you that my decision not to buy him a car was the right one for him at that time, and it sent a strong message about the importance of independence and self-sufficiency. In the long run, the decision strengthened our relationship.

Many parents feel that, because they are in a fortunate position financially, they therefore have an obligation to help their children. But I suggest that they try to let their kids make decisions and suffer the consequences – or enjoy the rewards. Kids need to understand the realities of life, or they may one day find themselves – when the parents either no longer can support them or are not around to do so – unable to take care of themselves.

At the right time, and when your kids are at the right age, share some of your financial struggles with your kids. Stability is important, but kids also need to learn how to work through challenges, including financial ones. Parents should share the struggles they've faced, so the kids know that it is normal and that this is how people go through life.

Don't create a bubble for your kids, especially if you are fortunate enough to be comfortable financially. Your kids should understand that there are many people in the world who have far less and who struggle far more. Help them learn to distinguish essentials from nonessentials or luxuries and to choose essentials that are calibrated to their means. It's essential to have a way to get to work, but it's not essential that your transportation be a Porsche 911.

Sometimes dysfunctional spending patterns are generated by underlying personal or family issues, and these difficulties may date back to your childhood or even to patterns established by earlier generations – your grandparents' attitudes and decisions may echo through your parents' lives and your own life. Even though the problems may be financially related, they sometimes go deeper than we as financial advisors can or should handle. In those situations, we may suggest that the family get some help from a counselor, especially when there is a complex family dynamic and a long history of imprudent financial behavior. Look at your finances and spending habits in a clear-sighted way, and, if necessary, seek advice from professionals who can help you work through personal or family barriers that may be preventing you or your kids from getting on firm financial footing.

Getting Your Kids Off the Payroll

If your kids have benefited from your generosity all their lives and into adulthood, they probably take your contributions for granted and may not understand how much that is adding up to. If that is the case, it's incumbent on you to make them aware and to gradually wean them off your assistance.

When kids are younger, in their late teens or of college age, you can insist that they pay for the things they want, while you continue to supply the things they need; the exercise of separating wants from needs is one that they can continue to use throughout their lives and is especially helpful in lean financial times, such as after a layoff or when starting a business. Ask kids to think through why they "need" something and ask them how much they will be willing to pony up for it. Knowing how to determine which items are "luxuries" and how to do without them, if necessary, is a valuable life skill.

If you are providing substantial support to adult children – those in their mid-20s or older – it is time to step back. Look together at the financial assistance you give on a monthly or annual basis, and identify the things you will begin cutting back. For example, you might start by removing your adult child from your cell phone plan. Or perhaps you can transfer car payments to your child. Don't pull the rug out all at once – instead, expect that your child will gradually take financial responsibility for his own bills over the course of a year or two, depending on the amount of help you've been supplying. Make a plan that, over time, shifts any payments you have been making on your child's behalf – for vehicles, insurance, rent, college loans, incidentals – to your child.

Think of yourself as a safety net for your kids rather than as a permanent source of help. Getting your adult children off the payroll protects your retirement assets, certainly, but more importantly it strengthens your kids' ability to manage their own lives and prepares them fully to embrace the future.

Tips for Family Gifting and Loans

- Make gifts random, in both amount and timing, so kids don't feel entitled to them or come to rely on the cash.

- Don't attach strings to gifts. If you choose to give your child money or a valuable item, give it freely and do not use the gift to manipulate your child.

- If you want to lend money to your children, make the loan professional and documented.

- Give or lend only within your means.

CHAPTER 3

Graying Divorce

Rick and Renee are great clients and have been for more than twenty years. Our firm started working with them a few years before Rick retired, and in addition to helping them with their investments, planning for their retirement, and preparing their taxes over these many years, we have been there for them through some challenging personal and financial periods. Several years ago, they moved to a wonderful community in Dallas, Texas, but were flying to Virginia for a few days to review their investment portfolio and discuss some matters related to their estate planning.

Renee called a couple of days ahead of the meeting to chat before they arrived, and to my great surprise she told me that she and Rick were divorcing. She said she wanted to advise us before the meeting, so we could discuss the financial impact the divorce would have on both of them. The two were in agreement about the divorce and wanted to do what was right and best for both of them. This call was a shocker. Not because we haven't received news like this before – we have, many times – but I was a bit thrown this time because I'd always thought these two were so compatible and happy together. It can be difficult to know what is going on inside a marriage – sometimes, even for the couple.

Dazed and Confused

One day, your husband (or wife) comes home and says, "I want a divorce." Maybe you saw it coming. And maybe you didn't.

Your stomach lurches. Your head spins. Perhaps you think it's a phase or a passing dissatisfaction that will not ultimately be fatal to your marriage. Or maybe you've known for a while, deep down, that it really is over, and the moment you've been dreading has finally arrived. But even if things have seemed off for a while, even if the two of you haven't been connecting in recent months (or years), the announcement can come as a shock.

The fact is, it's happening more and more among Baby Boomer couples. While divorce rates overall have leveled off, and have even begun to decline among some demographics, they've risen among Americans over 50 years of age, with approximately 25% of the divorces today occurring among couples who are 50-plus.

> The chances of an adult over 50 divorcing doubled between 1990 and 2014, and the jump was even higher for those over 65.[1]

And when couples divorce in their 50s, 60s, or 70s, there is less time to recover from the experience – not only emotionally, but financially as well. The marriage may be decades old, or it may be a second or even third marriage of shorter length; either way, the fallout can be devastating. Just as you are beginning to think about slowing down and enjoying life, about giving up the demanding schedule built around advancing in a career or raising children, a wrench is thrown into the works. For a spouse caught off guard by the announcement, the revelation can be shocking. You're nearing the goal you've both been working toward for years, if not decades, and now this? Even the spouse who suggested the divorce may be left reeling.

Why This? Why Now?

The reasons people divorce later in life mirror the reasons younger couples break up, and can include relationship problems such as infidelity or alcohol abuse. Often, though, the couple (or one half of the couple) simply feel that they have grown apart and are no longer in love – and such feelings take on new urgency as they hit milestone birthdays in their 50s, 60s, or beyond.

We all look around us at magazines and newspaper articles or at social media or other popular-culture influences, and the message we see over and over is that it's never too late to be what you want to be; it's never too late to pursue your true passions. People are living longer and are healthier and more active into their later years than they ever have been before – the average life expectancy in the United States in 2015 reached 78.8 years of age for men and 81.2 for women.[2] And as people live longer, their expectations for what later life looks like have changed. As Americans, we place a high value on fulfillment and feel entitled to our own happiness, no matter our age. If the marriage is not working, we may decide we don't want to live out the next 20, 30, or more years with someone we don't love.

Of course, reaching a certain phase of life – and retirement itself – can force us to some sharp realizations. When you retire and the children are out of the house, you and your spouse will likely spend a lot of time together. Without the activities that surround taking care of kids and the structure of regular work life to distract you, you may realize that you long ago lost the thread of your relationship.

As we reach a certain age and as divorce has become more socially acceptable overall, some of us care less about what our friends and social circle think. And with kids mostly or fully grown, we worry less about how a split will affect them. With only so much time left to us, we wonder if we can be happier and healthier – and perhaps even find new love – if we take a bold step. If we decide that the fabric of the relationship can't be mended – or that it's not worth trying to repair – we may choose to end the marriage.

Changing times, too, bring a new range of possibilities. Over the past few decades, greater options for women in the work world have led many to seek independence if they are unfulfilled or are suffering abuse from a spouse. Financial independence encourages other types of independence. Women who are tied to a husband's finances with few resources of their own may be less likely to ask for a divorce.

According to the National Center for Health Statistics, approximately 80% of divorces are initiated by women.[3]

First Things First

Let's face it. Divorce is not a topic couples want to talk about. They probably don't want to talk about it with their friends or their families, and they would certainly prefer not to discuss it with a financial advisor, divorce attorney, tax specialist, or other professional. No one wants to look down the road and contemplate the realities of a split, so there can be a tendency to ignore the signs or to put off dealing with the practical details. You have enough to do holding it together emotionally during such a stressful time. But there are steps your financial advisor and other professionals can take to make sure both you and your spouse (and any children you may have) are well taken care of, and the sooner those plans are begun, the smoother the process will be.

In my more than 30 years as a financial advisor, I have received dozens of phone calls from clients who confide that their marriage is on the rocks. Sometimes it's a surprise, and other times I've had some warning. The first thing I say is, "How can we help?" This initial conversation is an opportunity to find out where the person is in terms of his (or her) thinking and to see how he is doing – and also to find out where the spouse is and how she is doing. Often, when people are divorcing, one spouse leads the effort, and it's good to know who that is. I've found that it's rare for divorce to be a completely mutual decision, and the fact that the two are not on the same page may create problems when it comes time to make decisions.

I like to check in on the kids, too, and ask how they are dealing with the news. If the kids are young – college age or younger – the situation can be complex, because there will likely be the issue of financial support for them and the matter of financing their college educations, as well as possibly thorny issues of custody or visitation. But divorce affects the family even when the children are older, and adult children's reactions can also create difficulties for divorcing couples. While there is no child support or visitation to deal with per se, the split may leave the children shocked or upset. If the sale of the home they grew up in is involved, they may face deep feelings of loss, realizing that the center of their childhood life, and the site of holiday celebrations and other family traditions, will soon be gone.

A number of adult children may be depending wholly or partially on the financial support of (or even living with) their parents. This makes the divorce even more complicated both from a financial perspective and in terms of the family dynamics. Adult kids, like younger children, may feel greater allegiance to one parent, especially if one wants the divorce and the other does not, leading to feelings of anger or guilt. Balancing relationships with both parents, together with negotiating any competing opinions of siblings, can lead to a lot of family tension.

Taking the emotional temperature of the situation helps me prepare for the way the scenario might unfold and offer the kind of help the couple is likely to need. I might ask if they have sought counseling and if there is any hope of reconciliation. This can give me some idea of the likelihood that matters will indeed progress and also provides some sense of the timeline. Whatever the answer, it tends to be a slow process; a very efficient divorce might take 9 to 12 months, but the more normal course is two to two-and-a-half years or more. The more complicated the financial scenario and the more difficult the family dynamics, the longer the divorce will take. Some clients are able to manage the entire process amicably and with a great deal of respect for each other, but I've also seen cases where things got very nasty.

Our role, as financial advisors, is to provide our clients with objective information about their finances and the impact different scenarios will have on their financial future – and also to bring some sanity to the process. Because the dissolution of a marriage is such an emotional topic, tensions can run high even in the most cordial of circumstances. We help people step back and look at their financial options calmly and in a way that will lead them to more thoughtful decisions.

Preparing for your meeting with your financial advisor will help him or her offer you the best advice tailored to your situation:

- Be as open and honest about the divorce as possible; if you are comfortable doing so, share your personal needs and expectations for what will happen during the divorce and postdivorce.
- Share all your financial information; this includes tax returns, financial statements, income and expenses for the past year, and insurance policies.
- Write down any future expenses you anticipate, such as education for children or grandchildren, major home repairs, family health issues, new car, and so on.
- Review estate documents for necessary changes along with changes in beneficiary designations on retirement plans and life insurance policies.
- Be prepared to discuss your personal and financial goals, both short term and long term, such as moving to a new home, starting a business, changing jobs, or retiring.

A Climate of Trust

Over years of working with our clients we build warm and trusting relationships, and yet sometimes our clients still surprise us when they confide marital tensions that had been bubbling below the surface. My colleague Gary Ingram had been working with a couple for many years and had a well-established relationship, when one day the wife, Abby, called to say that her husband had asked her for a divorce. They'd just been in the office and everything seemed fine. In fact, a month earlier the couple had agreed to go to a Washington Capitals hockey game with Gary and his wife. It was hard to even believe.

Abby was in a bit of a tailspin and wanted to immediately change the beneficiary on her account. We told her that was completely under her control, but when she needed money coming out of a joint account, we would need to involve both of them, and we'd like to have joint communication as soon as possible. We got the two together in our office and laid out some options for them. We wanted to get immediately to a place of transparency, and we asked them both to agree that if either asked us to withdraw money from a joint account, or if we noticed money moving around that we didn't initiate, that it was okay to convey that information to both of them. While that was a difficult moment because of the hurt feelings and distrust between the couple, they agreed.

On the first call, Abby volunteered that she wouldn't be attending the hockey game, and Gary assured her that he'd need to decline as well, of course, and that it wouldn't be appropriate under the circumstances. Over the next few months Gary had several calls with each of them, and about once a month reached out to make sure both were doing okay. Eventually, he decided to set up lunch with each separately, with no agenda, just to touch base. An e-mail invitation went to each separately, and he heard almost immediately from Tom, the husband, accepting and setting up a time and place for lunch. But he never heard from Abby. When Gary and Tom confirmed, however, Tom said that Abby would be joining them, and that the two had reconciled.

So this is a divorce story that didn't end in divorce, and it's proof of what patience and honesty and time can sometimes solve. If the two had ultimately chosen to proceed with the divorce, they'd laid good groundwork for a process in which they would be best served by trusting each other and the professionals to arrive at an equitable settlement. When people are faced with a difficult situation, they don't always behave at their best, but Abby and Tom committed to transparency and fair dealing even at their most vulnerable moment.

When the End Is Inevitable

Once a couple has come to a firm decision to divorce, things usually get a lot more tense for the two of them. At that point, they're not figuring out whether they will survive as a couple; they are trying to see their way forward separately, as individuals – and sometimes those individual interests are in conflict. While a couple may have enough in retirement assets to support them comfortably, a split of the assets, paired with the fact that those same assets must now support two households rather than one, can strain the budget and change the realities of the individuals' lifestyles.

I have known Bob and Kitty for what seems like forever. Bob, a marketing executive, is a hard-driving person who enjoys his success, although he likes to complain about how hard he is working and the long hours his job entails. Kitty worked as a nurse until they had children and then stayed home to raise the kids. She often talked about going back to her career and how much she missed working.

Kitty and Bob's relationship had lost its sizzle many years earlier, and now the marriage seemed mainly functional, concerned with raising kids and maintaining a home, interspersed with a vacation here and there. To no one's surprise, when they reached the age of 54 and the kids were out of the house, they decided to separate. I knew from the beginning that Bob and Kitty were going to have a hard-fought divorce and that no one was going to be happy until it was over and they could finally move on. I was right.

The signs of trouble were abundant. First, splitting their assets meant that there wouldn't be enough to maintain two households and two separate sets of living expenses. Both would need to continue working; Bob's plan to retire at age 60 was now a distant dream. Second, the two came from different backgrounds. Bob was from an upper-middle-class family and would eventually inherit some assets, while Kitty was unlikely to have any future inheritance. The hard economic reality both would face post-divorce is probably part of the reason they stayed together for so long – neither wanted the change in lifestyle that was sure to follow a split, and they knew that the process itself would be painful.

We pulled together a list of assets they considered marital property and those they considered separate property (more about this in a moment). Of course, Bob thought that some of the property he received as gifts from his family should be kept separate and excluded from marital property, while Kitty felt strongly that they were marital assets.

There are rules for which assets are considered marital and which are considered separate, but there are also a number of caveats that can make the distinction murky. Typically, when an asset is received as a gift or through inheritance, it is considered separate property. But if you change the title of the property and then put it in a joint account and use the assets for joint living needs, it may be considered marital property. The determinations depend on the state in which you live, which is why, as we will see, a divorce attorney familiar with the laws of the state is so important.

Because Bob and Kitty couldn't agree on how to categorize the assets or on how long Bob should pay spousal support, the case went in front of a judge, who ruled that all assets titled jointly were marital property. In addition, the judge ruled that the marital assets would be split 70/30, with 70% going to the wife and 30% to the husband. That was considered an equitable distribution in the eyes of the court.

Can a 70/30 split really be an equitable distribution of assets? Well, yes it can, as we'll see shortly, and in Bob and Kitty's case that was the outcome. Because of the generous asset split, Bob only paid spousal support for five years. According to our calculations, this meant Bob could retire in a modest home at age 65. That is five years later than his initial goal, but, as Bob says, work is good for the soul. Kitty will eventually need to sell the home and reduce her monthly expenses, unless she returns to work.

Although the divorce was extremely stressful, Bob and Kitty are both happier, the kids are happier, and they are getting along fine in their new, more modest lifestyles.

The Basics of the Asset Split

A spectrum of arrangements and resolutions exists, from informal, mutually agreed separation all the way to litigious divorce, as we saw with Bob and Kitty. If you can come to an amicable agreement, you will save yourself a bundle in professional fees. As the old joke goes, in a divorce you can split the assets in half or in thirds – with a third going to attorneys and other professionals. Perhaps as critically, avoiding protracted fights and nasty court battles over property and other matters saves a great deal of emotional wear and tear.

Because all 50 states now have some form of no-fault divorce, a divorce can proceed with no requirement to assign blame or provide evidence of a party being at fault. When there's no fault, division of assets, as well as support, if any, is typically the main issue. State law governs division of assets, but there are many ways to slice and dice the property within the framework of the law. And in states that recognize fault divorces, when there is a finding of fault (if one spouse alleges an extramarital affair or a substance abuse problem on the part of the other, for example), the finding may affect the division of marital property or award of support.

The steps for property division in most divorces follow the same path. This process is carried out with the help of financial and legal advisors, with assistance from the courts where necessary:

1. List assets and debts.
2. Determine how the assets are titled.
3. Value the assets.
4. Determine the net after-tax value of each asset.
5. Divide the assets and debts.

List Assets and Debts

With the clients' help, we pull together a list of all their assets that is as accurate as possible. That includes financial portfolio, retirement accounts, real estate holdings, vehicles, art and antiques, jewelry – anything of value that the couple owns.

We also assemble a list of debts, which can include mortgages, car loans, credit card debt, student loans, personal loans, and business debt, among others.

Determine How the Assets Are Titled

As we saw earlier with Bob and Kitty, property is either marital (joint or community property) or nonmarital (sole or separate property). The way an asset is characterized (who owns the property) determines what happens to it after the divorce. Most states allow spouses to keep their separate property and divide joint property, although some have a "mixed" or "quasi-community" property category that allows the court to consider some assets to be, for practical purposes, joint marital property. (Your divorce attorney will be on top of the laws of your state.)

Marital property, unsurprisingly, is property acquired during the marriage, including money that either of you earned during the marriage and any property bought with that money. Separate property means assets that each person brought with him or her when the couple married, or that a person inherited or was gifted during the marriage, if it was given to the person singly.

If property is bought using separate funds, then the property is considered separate, assuming that the person is sole owner on the title. An illiquid asset that is inherited, such as a house (especially when it is inherited jointly, with siblings, for example), may create some problems for the owner, though. Even if the property is clearly separate and will remain with the person who inherited it, that asset may impact other noninherited property – the spouse who holds that separate inherited property may have to give up something else to offset the property, so that the division remains equitable.

Laws in this area are complex, and there are many caveats and exceptions regarding the way that property is characterized. Often, commingling of assets during a marriage can complicate the picture – sometimes the mixing of property is intentional but other times it may not be, as when a gift to one spouse is deposited in a joint account, for example. Prenuptial and postnuptial agreements, too, can change the determination of an asset – in fact, that's why they exist. These contracts can clarify financial responsibilities, protect a spouse from the other spouse's debts, and assure that property remains separate so that it can pass to children from a previous marriage, among other things.

Value the Assets

Valuation is pretty straightforward for assets such as bank accounts or stock holdings; a date is set (typically either the date of separation or the date of the formal division of property), and the balance of accounts on that date represents the value.

For most couples, the house and retirement accounts make up the lion's share of their assets, though a family-owned business may also represent a large portion of assets. The home is, perhaps, the most emotionally charged property. While an appraiser or real estate broker can give an assessment of what a home would be worth on the open market (together with an estimate for any costs associated with a sale), particularly if a couple has spent many years in a house and raised their children there, it represents more than the dollar value would indicate.

For older couples, a home's value may be somewhat different from purely the fair market value. For example, there may be local property tax breaks available to older people who own their homes, or property value increases may be suspended or discounted at a certain age threshold. In high-income brackets, especially, there may also be federal tax exclusions that make owning real estate attractive. Because each situation is different, the tax consequences need to be evaluated by a tax professional who is familiar with the couple's particular circumstances.

Late-life divorces can have particular impact on retirement assets. More mature couples, or those who have spent time in public-sector careers, may have defined benefit plans, often called pension plans, which can be complicated to assess depending upon a variety of factors, including early retirement incentives. For certain other retirement vehicles, such as 401(k) plans and individual retirement accounts (IRAs), the current value may be clear, determined by the account balance on a given date. If a spouse earned part of the retirement benefits before being married, however, that portion may be considered separate property in the event of a divorce.

Different states calculate the value of the separate property amount of retirement assets in different ways; some, for example, look solely at the amount in the account on the date of the marriage or include with that amount the interest and growth that have accrued over the period of the marriage. The portion that is determined to be separate property is then deducted from the value of the account, and the remainder is divided between the spouses in accordance with their settlement agreement or the judgment.

The value of retirement accounts must also be based on whether the contributions were made pre- or posttax. Plans for withdrawal are important, too, as income taxes are due on money withdrawn from tax-deferred accounts. Depending upon the type of account and the age of the contributor, penalties may also apply – to avoid the 10% penalty assessed by the Internal Revenue Service (IRS), the person must be fifty-nine-and-a-half at withdrawal. However, 401(k) plans operate a bit differently; if the person retires or is fired at age 55 or older, the money can be withdrawn without paying the IRS penalty. Some of the rules regarding distributions can be a bit tricky, so talk to your certified public accountant (CPA) or Certified Financial Planner™ (CFP®) professional.

We had clients who were divorcing, very amicably, and they had a lot of different types of assets: Brokerage accounts, IRAs, a deferred annuity, and the husband's pension. The couple was willing to say, you take this one and I'll take that one, but each asset had a very different tax implication. It may not be quite apples to oranges, but it's oranges to tangerines. The two assets may look very similar, but there are some features that make them different, including tax impact, liquidity, and required distributions. We ended up splitting every position 50–50 down the line for that couple, eliminating the various complexities.

A business is among the trickiest assets to value, in part because the contribution of each spouse to the business may be viewed very differently by each party, and because the value of the business may be perceived very differently by each as well. There are several ways to value a business, and the right method depends upon the type of business and its history – a tech start-up will likely be valued differently than a long-established meat-packing plant. A business appraiser, with input from both parties, will examine the business – its assets and liabilities as well as its potential for growth – and issue a report on the value of the business. You can save significant expense if you and your spouse agree on an expert and choose to abide by the valuation issued. If, however, the process has been contentious and there is serious doubt about how the valuation will be carried out, it may be worth hiring your own business appraiser to make sure your interests are well represented.

Divide the Assets and Debts

Once the value of assets has been determined, they can be divided, and, as with other aspects of divorce, state laws determine how marital property can be split. While some states require a 50–50 split, others seek "equitable" division – as was the case for Bob and Kitty. This means that the assets are not split evenly by the spouses but that the division takes into account other matters, such as whether one spouse has a disability or serious illness, whether one has supported another through school, and the earning capacity and amount of separate property of each of the spouses. If one spouse has put a career on hold to attend to the needs of family and thus has a much lower potential to earn, that may be reflected in the division of assets in an equitable arrangement. Fault, too, as I mentioned earlier, may play a role in the asset split in states that recognize fault divorces.

Unfortunately, it can be hard to determine what is truly equitable in such circumstances, and it can take many, many conversations before we get to an arrangement that everyone feels is fair. In some instances, the courts decide. The larger emotional matters that arise in the divorce may get played out on the financial field. Often, one spouse feels left behind and that the whole situation is unfair. Especially when the divorce was the other person's idea and that person goes on to thrive in life after the divorce, that success can be hard for the other to take.

Some assets are easily split down the middle at the time of divorce, but others are more complicated. A house, for example, might be retained by one spouse via a buyout; it might continue to be jointly owned by both spouses for some period (especially if children are still living at home and the family wants to maintain continuity for them); or it might be sold and the proceeds split. The best decision depends a great deal on the age and income of the couple and on their ability to agree to a plan that both feel is fair. Whatever the decision, it should be formalized in writing with a property agreement.

Handling the mortgage can be a challenge because the debt goes with the house and the new owner may not qualify for the mortgage individually. Ownership of debt is an important issue, as debt is not transferable between spouses or partners, it usually has a time period for payoff, and the payments can be variable. Decisions about how you divide the debt are as important as those about dividing the assets.

Retirement funds, depending upon the type, may be divided at the time of the divorce via a lump-sum payout or may be divided when the plan participant retires. Private retirement plans are governed by a federal law called the Employment Retirement Income Security Act of 1984, or ERISA. This law requires that divorcing couples file a qualified domestic relations order, or QDRO, which outlines the rights of a person to a portion of the retirement benefits his or her former spouse earned through participation in an employer-sponsored retirement plan. The order becomes "qualified" through its acceptance by the plan administrator. QDROs are integral to the division of a pension plan, and may be required for the division of a defined contribution plan (a 401(k) or similar plan); this is information that the plan administrator supplies. Don't make the mistake of taking a distribution from the pension plan or 401(k) plan before the QDRO is filed and accepted, as this may create serious tax implications for the person taking the distribution.

Businesses are typically awarded to the person who runs the business, and that person will either buy the other spouse out or designate property of similar value to be awarded to the less involved spouse. Occasionally, both spouses are integral parts of the business. If the divorce is amicable, it may be possible for both to continue in the business; otherwise, if an agreement cannot be reached, protracted legal wrangling is the likely outcome, with a court deciding how the matter should proceed.

Even when assets are supposed to be split down the middle, complicated valuation and differing tax consequences can make matters difficult. Intellectual property, for example, copyright of a book or a patent for a product, can be tricky to value; in some cases, the income is not generated until after the divorce, even though the work may have been done during the marriage, entitling the spouse to a share. Future income streams and retirement assets can be messy, and must be worked out on a case-by-case basis in a way that is fair to both parties. As you can see, dividing assets can be a complex process, so make sure you are getting the proper advice and guidance along the way.

Proceeding After the Split

If a couple doesn't have much in assets, the process of dividing property can be a little easier, but it isn't always. When one party feels that the division of assets, or even just the circumstance, is unfair, they may not want to let go. When that is the mind-set, it doesn't matter if they have a small amount of money or tens of millions. It's not about survival. There may be enough in assets for both to live very comfortable, even lavish, lifestyles, but the money becomes symbolic of the "final score." In a case that involves spousal support, the person who is providing the support and his/her attorney might say, "This amount of money is plenty." The other person and attorney may disagree vehemently. Deciding what "enough" means can be a very tricky proposition.

If you are going through a divorce, you should start building a separate cash-flow statement; each party to the divorce should have his or her own. Look carefully at all the assumptions – lay out the needs for the kids, house, necessities, lifestyle, and so on – and balance them against the assets you have. Put together a project plan for each person on how it could all work out. An advisor experienced in working with divorcing couples can be extremely helpful if you need assistance.

The financial plan you or your advisor create should include:

- A clear set of goals, objectives, and priorities.
- Current balance sheet (assets and liabilities).
- Current cash flow statement (income and expenses).
- Tax projection, filing jointly and separately.
- Projection of balance sheet, cash flow, and taxes for each person postdivorce.
- Financial independence projections for each person postdivorce.
- Life, disability, and health-care insurance analysis.
- Estate documents and beneficiary designations that should be reviewed with your attorney and your financial advisor.

Preparing the financial statements and postdivorce financial independence analysis is not the hard part; the difficulty comes from working through the analysis during this highly emotional period. In the end, we almost never see a settlement that everyone is entirely happy with, but we hope to see one that is fair to all parties. We do everything we can to make sure our client is protected and feels the outcome was ultimately just and reasonable.

One Divorce After Another

People who divorce tend to remarry. Statistically, these people are most likely to divorce again: The divorce rate for second and third marriages is even higher than the divorce rate for those who marry for the first time. For people in their 50s and early 60s, a previous marriage doubles the chance that they will divorce again; for those in the 65-and-up age group, the risk is four times higher.[4]

> The divorce rate for second marriages is 67%; for third marriages it is 73%.[5]

When people remarry too quickly after a divorce, they may be very likely to divorce again. Because they have not yet healed from the first relationship's bruises and may be seeking a quick fix for feelings of loneliness or unworthiness, they may rush into a new relationship. Their desire to fill the void can cause them to ignore red flags that would otherwise signal future problems. In addition, having been through one divorce, they know how to do it, in a sense. They've survived it once (or twice) before and figure they will survive again.

But if one divorce can cause a hit to a person's financial health, a number of divorces can blow it up entirely. We've had clients who have been divorced multiple times and who are paying spousal support and child support for each marriage. Even a person who is making significant money is going to have a hard time handling that scenario and is unlikely to ever enjoy a comfortable retirement.

When clients tell us they plan to marry or remarry, we help them think through their financial plans and we counsel them on the value of having a prenuptial agreement in place.

The Value of a Prenuptial (or Postnuptial) Agreement

One way to mitigate some of the financial ill effects divorce can have is to put in place a prenuptial or postnuptial agreement (now often called a premarital or postmarital agreement). These documents establish the rights of each spouse should the relationship end, laying the groundwork for spousal support, division of property, disposition of insurance, and all other financial and family matters in the event of a divorce. While no one wants to get married with one eye already squinting toward the possibility of divorce, it is worth setting out clear understandings, just in case.

If you've gone ahead and tied the knot already, it's not too late to create an agreement. A postnuptial agreement typically offers the same protections as a prenup, but is executed after the couple is married. Both prenuptial and postnuptial agreements are governed by state law, and provisions vary widely depending upon the state in which they are executed.

I had a client in her mid-50s who had sizable assets and was planning to get married. Her future husband was not as well off, so I strongly suggested a prenup. I've learned over the years that this is often a very difficult subject to bring up to the person you are in love with and hoping to marry. How do you approach the topic?

I suggested to my client that she explain to her future husband that her attorney and financial advisor both strongly recommended that the two of them have a document drawn up to make clear what would happen in the unlikely event of a divorce. Think of it like a catastrophic clause on your homeowners' insurance policy – you will probably never need to collect on it, but it is there in the unlikely event that something bad happens.

If you bring a prenup up with your future mate, the response may be, "Don't you trust me to do what is right and fair if something happens between us?" The appropriate reply is, "Yes, I know you love me and would do what is right and fair, but let's think it through now and be clear about what is fair. That way, in the unlikely event something should happen, we will be prepared."

My client and her future husband were able to agree, and her children – who were very happy their mom was getting remarried – were relieved to know that a prenup protected their mother if the relationship did not work out. The prenup provides clarity while everyone is feeling upbeat and rational. When storms come, fear often follows and our usual rational behavior may be nowhere to be found.

Here are a few suggestions as you consider a prenuptial agreement:

- Don't wait until the last minute to discuss a prenup with your future spouse. The attorneys we work with recommend the prenup be completed 30 days before the wedding; start discussing the matter early in the relationship, once you know you plan to marry. Be open and honest about your finances and why you feel a prenup document is helpful.
- Talk things over with your spouse-to-be before sitting down with the attorney who will draft the prenup. Write down the key points you agree and disagree on, and share them with your attorney and your financial advisor.
- Each spouse should have his/her own attorney, although one of the attorneys can be designated to draft the document.
- Both spouses should prepare a complete balance sheet of all assets, including jewelry and artwork, and all liabilities. They should also share tax returns for the previous year or two.
- A prenup is a very important legal document, so make sure you read and understand all of the provisions.

- There is no "perfect" agreement, and no one right way to decide what is right for you. This is your document, and it should outline what you both think would be fair should you divorce.
- The prenuptial may not address issues at death, so make sure your estate documents are completed as you would like, should either spouse pass away unexpectedly.

Sometimes Divorce Is a New Beginning

While we've focused, necessarily, on the difficulties of divorce and the ways that it can cause a retirement fail if you don't prepare adequately, the story sometimes has a happy ending. Even when an individual reduces his or her assets by half and pays spousal support, the divorce may ultimately be a positive thing.

I had clients, a married couple, who were both desperately unhappy in their relationship but were afraid of getting divorced because of the financial implications. They continued on that way for years, each making the other miserable the whole time, until finally they agreed it was time to separate. In the end, both realized how unhappy they had been and were thrilled to be living independently.

The wife kept the house and had enough money to be secure; the husband downsized from the home he had been living in, but he found a nice, comfortable place near his children and grandchildren. What they came to understand was that, although they each had only half the assets, they gained peace of mind, reduced their stress, had better relationships with their adult children and grandchildren, and found new freedom to be themselves.

No matter your age, divorce is an unwelcome topic. Whether it comes as a surprise or has been brewing for years, the breakup of a marriage creates upheaval in the lives of the couple, their children, other family members, and even friends and community members. And when a couple is older, there are challenges that don't appear (as much) for younger people. Priorities are different. Life experience is different, and your expectations for what lies ahead are different. With a little foresight, you can prepare for the consequences of a divorce, and, if that time should come, have a strong plan in place to ensure both you and your former spouse are well provided for.

Protecting Yourself in the Event of Divorce

- Prevent financial failure by putting a prenuptial or postnuptial agreement in place; this will bring clarity to property characterization, state intentions, and lessen conflict if you should divorce.

- Make sure assets are properly titled.

- If your child is getting married, encourage him or her to seek advice and consider a prenuptial agreement, so that assets passed down from you remain in his or her possession in the event of a divorce.

- If you find yourself facing a divorce, seek counsel from attorneys, financial advisors, and tax professionals who have had experience helping their clients through the process.

- Most importantly, be patient and take care of yourself. The process takes time and is very emotional, even under the best of circumstances. So take a deep breath, talk to friends who have had similar experiences, and set aside time to reflect on what is most important to you.

CHAPTER

4

That Home Away from Home

Shelly left me a brief voicemail message saying she and her husband, Steve, had seen a house for sale and they were thinking about buying it. That's exciting, I thought. But I was also curious because I knew they loved the home they were living in. Maybe they were thinking it was a bit too large, now that their children were grown and gone? Maybe they had decided that this was the time to downsize – to simplify their lives in a smaller place where they could walk to local restaurants and the beach?

I called Shelly back and she enthusiastically recounted all the high points of this home, which was just coming on the market and would sell quickly because it was a great place, in a great location. The real estate agent had told the couple they would have to act quickly if they wanted the house.

"So, Shelly," I asked, "are you planning to sell your other home and move?" "Oh no," she replied, "We are going to use the house occasionally on weekends, and then our kids and friends can stay there. It will be a great investment, Greg, but we need to act quickly. It is a great price, and both we and the kids love it."

Pinning Down the Fantasy

Who could blame Shelly and Steve for their excitement, really? It seems a simple dream. You're on vacation in Florida and you see a house for sale, right on the beach. Or maybe it's a gorgeous lake house or a cabin in the mountains where you like to ski. Wouldn't it make a great getaway, someplace you can go to leave the stresses of the workaday world behind? When you're ready, in 10 or 15 years, you'll retire there. After all, you love the area – and it will be a great investment, too! This house will be a wonderful place to host family gatherings, you think.

You will probably even save money in the scenario you are spinning because you'll be vacationing without having to pay the hefty prime-time rental rates and building substantial equity at the same time. Your kids, and in future years *their* kids, will be coming year after year to the beach house for joyous family vacations. When time has run its course or circumstances change, you can easily sell the house and make money. Or perhaps you'll leave the property to your children as a legacy, preserving memories of happy times and giving them a hub for multigenerational family get-togethers or a real estate jewel to sell if they wish. It's a win-win-win proposition.

If this is your thinking, you're not alone. An estimated 1.13 million vacation homes sold in 2014, representing 21% of real estate transactions.[1] But how many of those purchases end up matching the romantic view imagined by the eager homeowners?

It's not that such rosy scenarios never work out. They sometimes do. And even if the scene is not quite as picturesque as vacation home buyers first envisioned, there may still be good reasons to purchase that second home. We'll explore those reasons and assess how well the likely reality aligns with your overall goals. As financial advisors, our role is to help our clients come to their decisions with their eyes wide open, understanding the potential ramifications and possible downsides. Whatever decision they end up making, our aim is to help our clients take the greatest advantage of their assets and make smart financial decisions given their particular goals.

The first thing to think about is what you expect from your second home. How often will you use the home? Do you want it solely as a weekend or vacation property, for exclusive use by you and your family members? Are you buying it as an investment, expecting that it will greatly appreciate in value over the life of your ownership? Do you plan to rent it when you are not using it? Is this a place you plan to retire to? The answers to these questions will help you decide whether a second home is right for you and, if it is, how much you can afford.

Most people buying second homes have mixed motives, and often these motives are driven by emotion rather than pure reason. While buyers might plan to offset expenses by renting the house out when they won't be using it, they aren't necessarily choosing a house for its viability as a rental – and often they don't consider what renting out the property will involve.

When clients come to us and tell us they want to buy a second home, we first ask how frequently they are going to be using it. Think about what your current life is like and how you envision spending time at your vacation home. If you are not planning to spend at least two months out of the year at the home, you are generally going to be better off, financially, if you rent. If you expect to be living in the home for at least two months, we look at the costs and at your financial wherewithal. And if you are planning to use the home for four, five, or six months out of the year, we should definitely look at ownership.

Many people believe that real estate is always a good investment. When clients tell us that investment is a main driver in their desire for a second home, we suggest that we analyze the purchase over time (including all of the ongoing maintenance, insurance, taxes, and other costs involved in owning real estate) and compare it with other, easier-to-manage investment choices. Most clients are surprised when they see the analysis. Often, people think that real estate is a great investment but they forget that homes are what I like to refer to as "cost structures," meaning that houses require a lot of money to keep running properly.

Is It Really an Investment?

The sale price of the house is just the beginning of your expenses when you are buying a second home. But even the price can come as a revelation if you are looking in popular resort areas, where many desirable vacation homes are located. Forty percent of second homes sold are at the beach, while nearly 20% are in the mountains or on a lakefront.[2]

Closing costs and broker's commissions on high-priced real estate can add up as well – think back to the lengthy list of application fees, advance insurance payments, title search charges, inspection charges, and other miscellaneous fees that appeared on the settlement papers for your primary home. Your closing costs, when buying a home, are typically around 2 to 3% of the home's value; these costs are generally 6 to 8% when you are selling the home. So before you will make any money on your new investment, you need the home to appreciate around 10%. That is before we get into the costs of homeownership.

Ongoing maintenance can take a bite out of your budget. These expenses can easily mount to tens of thousands of dollars per year, and include repairs and regular maintenance, property taxes, and rising mortgage interest rates if you have an adjustable rate mortgage. Property taxes, too, may rise unexpectedly, depending upon the area. It's worth looking at the history of tax increases in the location you are considering, to make sure you know what the quarterly (or biannual) tax assessments are and that you're taking into account likely increases.

In addition, condominiums and homes in planned communities will almost certainly have maintenance fees, homeowners' association dues, and/or special assessments, which can total hundreds or even thousands of dollars per month, depending upon the site and the services provided. If homeowners' association dues don't cover lawn care and landscaping, snow removal, trash collection, and other such maintenance, you will need to arrange and pay for them on your own. Now add in monthly services such as gas and electricity, water, cable, and an Internet connection.

Next, take into account the fact that you must furnish and decorate your new home. Depending upon your tastes and your vision for your space, this can get expensive. In addition to furniture that suits your lifestyle in your vacation home, you will need another set of all the household items you find necessary: Sheets, blankets, and pillows; towels; dishes and flatware; pots and pans and other kitchen items; coffee maker; televisions; lamps; and so on. One expense that many don't consider is the leisure items you may want to keep at your vacation home, some of which may be duplicates of items you keep at your primary residence, including bicycles, fitness equipment, game tables, golf clubs, and other sports equipment.

Pam Schepis, an amazing interior designer – and my sister – notes that, assuming you are not planning to buy everything from Goodwill or Ikea, you should expect to spend around 10 to 20% of the home's value on the furnishings, window treatments, and other necessary items. Most of these items have little or no value when you go to sell the home, so now you need about a 20 to 30% gain upon sale of the home to cover your initial costs and the closing costs due upon selling.

You also need to get back and forth to your property, and the costs of travel can mount, especially if you are flying and are transporting a number of children or grandchildren. Costs such as hosting friends and extended family or loaning out your place should also be factored in.

The median distance between a vacation home and a primary residence is 200 miles. About 34% of vacation homes are more than 500 miles from the owner's primary home.[3]

Then you have insurance costs, and especially for properties along the water, where big storms often come through, the insurance can be extremely expensive – and sometimes even impossible to get. In 2017, several hurricanes and tropical storms devastated some coastal areas of the United States and the Caribbean, with photos of flooded and wind-damaged homes offering a sober reminder of the risks of ownership along the beautiful shoreline.

While you have your crazy periods of skyrocketing property values – the late 1990s, and the years from roughly 2003 to 2007, for example – when big gains are possible, home prices typically appreciate at about the rate of inflation, on an annualized basis: That is about 3% per year. And along with that 3% you have a lot of costs, as I've just pointed out. You will need to own the home for a long time if you are going to make money from its sale.

People tend to think, "I'm going to buy this house for $1 million and I'll use it and then sell it for $2 million in 10 years, and it will be this really great investment." That would represent a 7.2% rate of return if there weren't any expenses involved, and you would have doubled your money in 10 years, right? Well, not exactly.

Let's assume the following:

Purchase price = $1,000,000

Closing costs = $25,000 to $30,000

Annual costs over 10 years (taxes, insurance, maintenance at $20,000 to $30,000 per year) = $200,000 to $300,000

Home improvements and furnishings = $100,000 to $200,000

Selling costs ($2 million × 7%) = $140,000

Given this scenario, you will probably earn around $300,000 when you sell the house. That reflects an annual rate of return of only 2 to 3%.

What if, instead of purchasing that second home, you took the $1 million you were going to use to buy the house and invested it in a portfolio that yielded an annual return of 7.2%? Rather than owning your vacation home, you withdrew $25,000 each year from the portfolio to pay for a vacation rental home. How would your investment do over the 10-year period? In this scenario, you earn more than $630,000 after paying the rental expense, which gives you an annual simple rate of return of over 6%. Plus, you don't have to worry about hurricanes, maintenance, and other necessary upkeep.

As you can see, renting a home for a month or two will likely give you a better return on your investment than owning a second home will. If you were planning on renting a vacation home for more than two or three months, however, ownership may be a better financial decision, depending upon rental costs in your desired area and on whether you plan to rent the home out when you aren't using it. Each home purchase should be evaluated individually, as each scenario is different.

In most instances, the math of owning a second home is not as wonderful as you may have thought. But that does not mean that buying a vacation home is not the right decision for you. There may be many intangible benefits to having a second home, in terms of making memories with loved ones and simply enjoying life. These are things that have an emotional value that can't be calculated. At that point, we say it's not a pure investment, perhaps, but it's more of a lifestyle asset. It's okay to have lifestyle assets and to enjoy what you've worked so hard for. When making such a decision, it's smart to look at how something like a vacation home fits into your overall financial picture and think about what you want out of that home. In the end, you want to answer this question: Does it make more sense for me to own or to rent?

Is It a Lifestyle Asset?

The way we vacation is a lifestyle asset, just as our cars, our clothing, and our houses are all lifestyle assets, at least to some degree. A car is for transportation, yes, and a house is for shelter, but they also say something about who we are and what we value. Otherwise, we'd all be driving old jalopies that just get us from point A to point B and living in efficiency apartments. So above a certain level of utility, above the level at which the item performs its essential function, the style, amenities, and other add-ons are all benefits that we enjoy, that we feel add status, or that give us some other advantage.

As I said earlier, there's nothing wrong with having lifestyle assets, but as financial advisors, part of our job is to help you evaluate what you can really afford. Maybe a $500,000 home is better aligned with your overall goals than one that's $1 million. Or maybe any significant outlay is going to constrain other priorities in a way you won't be happy with. Our interest is in helping you figure out how to allocate assets so that one choice – in this case the decision to buy a vacation home – doesn't impede other goals, that is, your future financial independence.

When you are planning to sink money into a second home, you have to make sure you have enough in liquid assets to take care of your cash flow needs, and that will depend on your individual situation. Figuring out how much you can safely put toward your second home means examining your current home expenses, debt, and any other obligations such as child support and contributions toward retirement plans, and then balancing those financial obligations against your income. You need a realistic idea of how much you can spend on the house on a per-month basis, looking not only at the purchase price but at all the operating costs we discussed earlier.

Many people who contemplate a second home are either retired or are nearing retirement, so they are contributing to retirement funds as they prepare for post-work life. Especially if they are no longer earning a salary, we look carefully at the value of their liquid assets and the monthly "paycheck" they will need to draw from those assets to maintain the lifestyle they want to have. Liquid assets, for reference, are those you can easily sell and turn into cash, such as certificates of deposit (CDs), bonds, stocks, and mutual funds. Illiquid assets are assets that are harder to sell or that can take much longer to sell, such as real estate, private equity, or limited partnerships.

When considering a second home, think about how you see yourself using the new home and what else you would like to do. When you own a beach house, will you feel committed to going to the beach for all your vacations? Are you and your spouse (and your kids, if they are still at home) okay with that decision? Will you continue to take

Hawaiian vacations or European vacations as well? If so, we need to factor in those expenses. Will the second home be a replacement for other sorts of trips or will it be an add-on? It's better to think through all of these questions before you sign on the dotted line, so you have a clear idea of how much you can or should spend.

Thirty-eight percent of vacation home buyers pay for their properties with cash.[4]

Unfortunately, plans don't always work out the way you envision, so it's important to think through all your contingencies. In the summer of 2006, clients Jack and Joan were on vacation. While strolling the streets of Carmel-by-the-Sea, the pair fell in love with a beautiful property and quickly put in a contract. Because they planned on paying all cash, they were able to expedite settlement. Jack and Joan called my colleague Karen Tovey, excited about this new investment, and wanted our help in deciding which assets to sell so they could buy this lovely home.

The market was hot, and Jack felt like they had to buy right then or be shut out, so it was a somewhat impulsive decision. The couple splurged on this vacation home, figuring that they would move to it when they retired and in the meantime they would rent it out. The house needed some work in the kitchen and master bathroom, and then they had to furnish it. Given the rental market they were looking at, they felt they needed high-end finishes and furnishings, so they spent quite a lot getting the house ready.

Then the market fell apart due to the Great Recession and subprime mortgage crisis, and they weren't able to get the rental income they'd been hoping for. With the real estate crash, the value of the home dropped precipitously, and they were soon underwater in the house. At the same time, they decided that they didn't want to retire to California after all and they ended up selling the house. They aren't living under a bridge, but their ability to retire on the timeline they wanted was definitely impacted.

This is an example of the tremendous transaction costs if your timeline is too short. We have another client who bought a house very quickly and ended up selling just two years later. Even if the market remains healthy and prices are stable, the closing, moving, and furnishing costs are not recoverable. Just because you've fallen in love with a place and the prices are hot, don't jump into it. There will always be another house. As my dad used to tell me, there will always be another train coming along if you can be a little patient.

Real estate acquisition can become something of an obsession, especially in hot markets, and it can be tempting to get swept up in buying homes that turn out to be the wrong price, in the wrong location, at the wrong time. A partner of mine was working with a client who was quite wealthy. He'd sold a few businesses and done very well, and then bought several houses. Then the downturn of 2008 came and crushed him. He has been trying to wiggle his way out ever since and still hasn't made it back. One of the homes was his primary residence, while another was a vacation home, and a third was a home that he planned to retire to eventually. But cash flow got tight in the downturn and his assets were eroding, so he decided to sell . . . but he'd waited too long and ended up letting go of each home at a significant loss. Prices just didn't come back in the way he'd been hoping.

And that is another thing to think about when buying a vacation home. In uncertain times, luxury homes in resort areas are often not the ones that move, and prices can drop dramatically just as you need to unload your house.

We have a client with a second home in North Carolina at one of the resort areas. It is a stunning home, and the couple really enjoyed the time they spent there. They were aware when they bought the house that one day they would need to sell it to support their retirement, but they really wanted to have this great vacation home with good friends and a wonderful golf course nearby, so they went ahead with the purchase.

Unfortunately, the wife had a stroke and needed to move to a nursing home. It came time to sell the house to help support their finances, but the real estate market had not recovered fully after the Great Recession and now other, newer resorts were being developed, causing a significant drop in prices. Also, since it was a retirement-oriented area, many other residences were up for sale, as homeowners had either passed away or were moving to facilities that provided care. The home has been on the market for two years and will eventually need to be sold at a significant loss. This couple should be fine financially, but the pressure that has built as the house lingers on the market has been very stressful for them – certainly not the outcome they envisioned.

Retirement Home?

It's common for people to buy a second home, thinking they will use it as a vacation home or weekend retreat for a decade or so and then retire there. After all, they figure, they love the area and it will make good financial sense. But things don't always work out as planned.

Very few of my clients end up retiring to their vacation homes, even if that had been their intention. For one thing, vacations are typically about luxurious fantasies, where you spend your days relaxing on the beach, golfing, or getting a massage at the spa, and that may not fit the way you will live day to day in retirement. In addition, the things you need to live a long and healthy life in retirement may be different from the things you want when you are vacationing. For example, good medical facilities may not be at the top of your list for a vacation spot, but they can be critical in retirement should you or your spouse need care.

Another caution is that planning 10 or 15 years in advance is tricky; a lot of things can happen over that period. By the time retirement comes, interests have changed, the kids have grown up, neighborhoods have evolved, and you may not want to live in that place anymore. Possibly, a new locale has caught your eye, or maybe you've realized the downsides to the area.

Before you do buy for year-round living, you may want to see what the area is like in all seasons. If you are opting for a seasonal resort area, be certain that you will be happy living in a place that swells with vacationers in high season and may be somewhat lonely in the off-season. Does the climate suit you, and will you be close enough to friends and family? Does the community offer the types of activities you enjoy? While most of your days are taken up with working when you are preretirement age, you will have a lot more time to pursue your interests when you are no longer working.

We recommend that, before you buy a house in a particular location, you rent there for a few months to see if you and your partner like living in the area, to understand the pros and cons of the neighborhood, and to get a sense of whether it matches your dreams. Try a two-month rental; if it costs you $10,000 per month in rent but you discover that it's not a place you would really want to live, you've saved a bundle. That $20,000 looks like a bargain compared with the $1 million or more that a vacation home might run.

Weighing the Risk

When people are looking to make big decisions such as buying a second home, we, as financial advisors, do our best to lay out the analysis, to help sort through the pros and cons so that clients can make the best decisions for themselves. We certainly raise red flags where we see them, but there is never a guarantee of how things will turn out, one way or another. Some people are more cautious by nature, and others are more willing to take risks. When we lay out what we think is the likely financial scenario, about half of the clients will move forward and the other half will take a step back. If they were already unsure about the wisdom of the move they were considering, our analyses can sometimes push them back from the edge.

One client, a woman in her 60s named Maria, wanted to buy a beach house on Long Island. She was from a big family, and she pictured returning to the vacation spot she and her siblings had enjoyed as children and sharing that with the whole family. She wanted to pay cash, and the property would have been close to a million dollars. We looked at her finances from the perspective of whether she would be okay if she plunked that much down on a second home. Maria is living off her portfolio, and we can't control the market, so there is always the chance that a downturn will cause a problem. We advised that she could do it but things might get tight financially in her later years, and we might need to sell the property at that time. We asked Maria how important it was to her to purchase this home.

She was in no rush – she wanted to think through the decision to be sure that buying a beach house made sense for her. And then, in 2012, Superstorm Sandy hit the coasts of New York and New Jersey very hard, and the area where she had been planning to buy was devastated. Any home she would have purchased would surely have sustained major damage, if not been completely swept away.

When a client plans to buy a vacation home in the Caribbean or on the coast of Florida or the Carolinas, we know that hurricanes are a big risk, but a storm of that nature on the northeastern shoreline wasn't of huge concern. We have other clients with primary homes in those areas, and the losses, issues with rebuilding, and declining property values in devastated neighborhoods have wreaked a lot of havoc in their lives.

In this case, a loss of that magnitude could have created a major crisis if she'd needed cash, and Maria ended up relieved that she hadn't moved forward with purchasing a beach house. We try to plot out the worst-case scenarios without being a complete downer; it's worth looking at the worst that would happen if an asset completely disappeared, and then making a decision based on what you can afford to lose. Everyone is happy when they buy and the real estate market goes on a nice run and prices go up, but you can't count on that. So plan for the worst and hope for the best.

Partial Ownership

Sometimes, people decide that fractional ownership is a solution to the concern of taking on outsize financial or maintenance obligations. You can partner with others in owning the vacation home, sharing expenses and the tasks associated with ownership, while also enjoying regular vacations in your own home. Or perhaps you think that renting the place out for the months you are not there will offset the costs and make owning the home a worthwhile investment. Sounds like a great idea, right?

Unfortunately, these scenarios can be complicated to navigate, and I've rarely seen them work out well. If you and a partner (or more than one partner) are investing together, you definitely have to be on the same page with your co-owners about how you are going to handle issues surrounding the property. This can be tough because people look at life differently and they treat their property differently.

We've seen that some people have children or pets that behave well and some people have children or pets that, shall we say, *don't* behave well. You need to consider how you will feel if you find the property is not being cared for in the way you would expect, and about how that could affect your friendship with your partners. One family can afford to upgrade the property while the other can't or doesn't want to do it in the same way. One wants class A appliances and the other wants class B appliances, to say nothing of individual tastes about décor. Think of your siblings and how difficult it can be to sort out disagreements; it can be even tougher with friends. The whole thing can get very messy.

We had clients, a couple, who invested in a vacation house with several other couples. They were renting it out and each couple got a chance to use the house for a week or two, and all was going well. But then one of the couples broke up, which put a strain on the arrangement. The couple who broke up couldn't decide which spouse was going to get the property or who would pay the mortgage and other expenses, and soon nobody was happy. Eventually, all the co-owners decided to put the house on the market and they ended up selling it at a loss.

Some of the problems that occur with fractional ownership are magnified when you rent out your home; people staying for just a week or two won't have the same interest in caring for the property that a co-owner does, and while most guests will be respectful of your home and abide by house rules, some will not.

If you decide to go ahead and buy with a group of friends or rent the property out to offset some of the costs, we suggest that you consider hiring a property manager who can arrange for cleaning, landscaping, maintenance and emergency repairs, and, if you plan to rent the property, handle the screening of guests and collecting the rental fees. Don't underestimate the effort involved; managing a rental property is a lot of work, and the problems often come at the most inopportune time. Though the property manager represents a cost, the time and aggravation you save will likely be more than worth it. It might even save a friendship or a marriage! Even with a property manager, don't underestimate the time, effort, and cost involved in renting out your vacation home.

Is Vacation Home Ownership Right for You?

You've worked hard and planned carefully so you can enjoy your retirement, and that house at the beach, you think, is just what you need to make your dreams come true. If the home you are thinking about is within your range of affordability, is a place you plan to use frequently, and will serve as a beloved gathering place for family and friends over many years, it may be a lifestyle asset well worth having.

Step back and make sure you've considered all aspects of buying a second home before you go ahead. Crunch the numbers and talk to others who have purchased vacation homes before jumping in yourself. And if you determine that it's the right move for you, you will be able to sink your toes in the sand with the peace of mind that comes from a decision well considered.

Things to Consider When Buying a Second Home

- Do the math: What increase in home value will you need in order to break even when you sell, given all the costs you will incur? (Closing costs at purchase and sale, together with the cost of furnishings and maintenance costs, typically add 20 to 30% to the initial price of the home.) Looking at all the costs involved, calculate the increase in price needed in order for you to make a 7% return on your investment.

- Decide the primary purpose of the home – is it a lifestyle asset or an investment asset?

- Evaluate the impact this purchase will have on your monthly and annual spending; don't forget to include the remodeling and eventual replacement of the roof and appliances, along with ongoing maintenance and repairs.

- If you are investing with friends or family, outline in a document a philosophy and process for using and managing the property. Be clear on how you will handle the property when one party decides they want out.

CHAPTER 5

The Lure of the Entrepreneur

You've had a rich and varied career filled with achievements and monetary rewards, and now you plan to sit back and enjoy the fruits of your labor. This is the golden time you've been waiting for, and you're looking forward to exploring new hobbies and spending more time with friends and family. But after a few months of much-needed rest and relaxation, you're bored. You value your new freedom yet feel like you are stagnating as you spend your time reading the news, playing tennis, or puttering around the house – you realize that you like being *in* the game, not on the sidelines. Maybe it's time to retire from retirement?

A while back, I was playing in a charity golf tournament with Harry and Jim, and they both told me they had tried to retire a couple of times. Harry explained, "You know, I retired once already and I am having to figure out how I can retire again. We have over a hundred employees and other businesses counting on the work we do."

When Harry retired the first time, in his late 50s, he thought he would start a small consulting firm and maybe hire a couple of people to support his work. As luck would have it, the business took off. Not one to miss an opportunity, he kept growing the company and now has offices around the world, and is busy traveling and working 50- and 60-hour weeks, not something he had expected to be doing in his mid-70s.

There are people who enjoy working long hours, even in their late 60s and 70s. But sometimes they get stuck on the merry-go-round and can't seem to get off, even if their life is not quite what they want it to be. Although Harry may not have as much free time as he sometimes wished, he didn't regret starting his business. His work supported who he was and gave him an identity as a successful CEO and entrepreneur, and that made him feel good. Harry's family would have liked to spend more time with him, but, overall, they supported his work and his desire to stay in the game.

Jim wasn't quite so lucky. After he retired for the second time from a career as a marketing executive, a close friend came to him to discuss a business idea. Jim had been very successful in his career, and a friend thought they would be great business partners. Jim said, "At the time, I was full of energy and got excited thinking about building a new, cutting-edge business."

The business idea was for a cool new home safety product, which required design engineers, a manufacturer, and a distribution and sales system. All of those areas must be executed well if the business was to be successful. At the beginning, everyone was gung-ho, and Jim agreed to act as CEO and to finance the business.

I asked Jim if a financial advisor or his accountant helped him analyze the business structure or had provided financial analysis. He said no but that he and his partner had prepared some initial projections and built a business plan. Given the tone of his voice, I realized that this business did not end well, so I asked Jim a few questions out of curiosity: Were there other investors helping to support the business financially? Did you or your partner have experience building a start-up business and manufacturing a product? Most importantly, since you are currently retired, were you able to protect your financial independence?

We had a great conversation, and I learned a lot about what could and did go wrong. Sadly, Jim lost more than $1 million before he and his partner realized that they had to shut the business down. He told me, "I am retired, but my wife and I are not at the comfort level I thought we would be at this time in our lives."

Be Careful How You Step In

If your work life has been go, go, go for decades, stopping suddenly can be difficult. After all, you're shifting from a workday in which nearly every minute of your time is scheduled and you are in constant demand to a daily routine in which you may have nothing of great consequence to do, no place to be, and no one counting on you for your insight or acumen.

Your first thought when confronted with such restlessness may be, "I'll get a job, something less demanding, or possibly I'll start a business!" It's exciting to think about new ventures, to look forward to building a business that combines your interests and your strengths. And many people in retirement have a great deal of vision and talent to offer, as well as time. Embarking on a second act as an entrepreneur or self-employed business owner is increasingly common, as people remain healthy and active often late into their lives. Starting a business can be a great way to use your time and energy and to earn additional income, which may be especially welcome if you've retired early, either by choice or because of restructuring in the company you worked for.

> In 2016, the *Kauffman Index of Startup Activity* found that roughly 24% of new entrepreneurs were aged 55 to 64, up from 15% in 1997.[1]

There are numerous pitfalls associated with business start-ups, however, and these can derail your retirement savings if you are not mindful of them, jeopardizing your future financial independence and threatening your peace of mind. Fifty-five percent of businesses fail in their first five years,[2] often because the entrepreneur lacks the skills or experience to run the company or because he has allowed emotions to cloud his judgment. In these cases, the business may have been poorly positioned to succeed from the outset or may have started strong but spiraled downward, and the business owner is so invested that he doesn't know when to quit. Having a strong plan can not only limit your exposure financially but also ensure that you have the pieces in place to give your fledgling company the best chance for success.

Have a Solid Plan

When zeal untethered from reality meets lack of experience and preparedness, a host of problems can ensue. One client's experience offers a case study in the things that can go wrong – and allows us to look at how the business could have been better organized and launched.

Dan had made a lot of money as a manager at a multinational pharmaceutical company; he'd worked hard, been in the right place at the right time, and done very well with his stock options. He then retired at a relatively young age, choosing to move back East, to a part of the country where he and his wife had grown up. There, they could raise their kids near family and old friends, and enjoy life at a slower speed.

Perhaps unsurprisingly, given his young age and previously demanding job, Dan found the pace *too* slow and began to grow bored. Finding another traditional job did not interest him – he'd done the daily grind in a corporation for decades already and knew he didn't want to deal with the hierarchy, pressure, and long hours that came with work in a big company.

Dan's level of wealth allowed him some flexibility – he didn't need to bring in a great deal of money because his portfolio would support his family's lifestyle – and he had lots of ideas for innovative products in the health-care arena. He began to get excited about the multitude of possibilities, and envisioned a bright future with himself at the helm of a pioneering start-up that would ultimately change the way people stay healthy.

The next thing you know, Dan has started a new company, included a couple of partners who were interested in his idea, and sunk considerable cash into launching the business. While his idea for a health-tracker app showed promise, he was entering a rapidly burgeoning market and he had no background in running a start-up. Building a successful business from the ground up requires a set of skills quite different from those needed to manage people and projects at an established company, and it's a set of skills that very few people have.

In his exuberance, Dan moved forward quickly, taking on partners, hiring employees, and leasing space. Unfortunately, he didn't stop to consider the legal and financial ramifications of these decisions. Dan was moving fast, with great enthusiasm and energy, and soon things weren't going well for his company. With no formal partnership agreements in place, the responsibilities of the partners were unclear, and Dan's position as sole guarantor of the lease and other contracts left him vulnerable. He had not run a company before and didn't realize how easy it would be to get caught up in lawsuits with unsatisfied partners and investors when the business began to falter. Because he believed in his idea wholeheartedly, Dan found it impossible to know when to quit, and ended up losing hundreds of thousands of dollars instead of making hundreds of thousands, or even millions, as he had dreamed.

Five Qualities or Skills All Entrepreneurs Need

When a client comes to us and floats the idea of starting a business, we want to encourage him or her. After all, many people could use additional income to support the lifestyle they desire in retirement, and many have contributions they yet want to make to the world. We don't want to dampen the person's enthusiasm – but we do want to help her evaluate whether she has the experience and skills she needs to be successful as an entrepreneur. And we want to help her put boundaries around the venture so that assets essential to her long-term well-being are protected. Unfortunately, unbridled enthusiasm can be difficult to slow down and redirect.

My experience has shown me that not everyone has what it takes to flourish as an entrepreneur. After founding and running, with my partners, a thriving wealth advisory firm, I've learned that you need certain traits to do well. Here are five essential qualities or skills you must have if you are to succeed as an entrepreneur:

1. **You need to have a strong vision.** You must be able to see clearly what you want to build and have the passion to follow through on your goals.
2. **You must be a good decision maker.** As an entrepreneur, you will be responsible for executing your business plan; you must be able to generate a range of potential solutions to problems, evaluate all the options, and decide quickly and confidently on the course that will lead to the best outcome.
3. **You need to manage risk appropriately.** Starting a business is inherently risky – that's just the nature of entrepreneurship. But a successful entrepreneur knows how to evaluate risks and choose wisely, how to minimize the downside, and when to cut her losses.
4. **You must be a good listener.** Being open to the opinions and suggestions of others means that you will get greater insight into the strengths and weaknesses of your business and will get more feedback that can help you head off problems or generate solutions.

5. **You need to be a great communicator.** You have to be able to share your vision with others – partners, employees, investors, customers – and you must be able to effectively communicate goals and expectations for everyone in the company.

Before beginning any entrepreneurial venture, make an honest assessment of your skills. If you are deficient in one or two of the qualities on this list, you may be able to develop them, or you may find a partner who can fill in those gaps. You might also learn that you aren't well suited to the uncertainty of a start-up and would find another type of work more satisfying. Don't underestimate the pressures that come with entrepreneurship. You need to manage this stress properly, or it will spill over into your business and to your employees and your family.

Setting Up for Success While Minimizing Risk

After we listen to a client tell us about her business and why it is such a great idea, we explore with her the worst-case scenario, taking the role of devil's advocate. The client is often not prepared to answer the questions we pose, but the conversation gets her thinking about the business and the financial risk involved. It also helps draw a line in the sand; if she approaches that line, she should completely reevaluate whether it's worth going forward.

New entrepreneurs need to think through the business model for their venture and make a realistic assessment of the associated costs, which they tend to underestimate. It's also important to consider a few questions: What are the legal ramifications of the particular business, and what safeguards should you have in order to operate with a reasonable amount of risk? Who do you have in place to keep you accountable?

When you are working through your business model, think in terms of the five "P's"; if you can develop a written plan that incorporates these five essentials, you greatly increase your probability of success.

1. **Purpose:** This is your company's mission and set of beliefs. You and your partners and employees must be clear about *why* you are in business and *how* you will operate as you work toward your goals.

2. **People:** You need an understanding of the skills (both technical and soft skills) of people you need to be part of the business. Who will make good partners? Who will make good employees? You also have to understand the needs and aspirations of the people you are serving, your customers or clients.
3. **Process:** It is important to establish business processes that let you manage operations, scale the business, and work efficiently.
4. **Price:** Your pricing model must make sense for your business and also for your customers or clients. In order to develop a solid pricing strategy, you'll need to know your customer, tally your costs, assess your competition, and decide on how much revenue you need to, want to, or can generate.
5. **Profits:** Profits are, of course, linked inextricably with your revenue targets, and thus your pricing model. You should look realistically at what your opportunity for profit will be, given all the information you gather as you set pricing, and decide whether the investment is worth it.

Once you have your five P's in order and have determined that you're ready to move ahead, you can save yourself a lot of grief if you formalize agreements. Pro forma financial statements, clear operating agreements, proper employee contracts and work policies, vendor agreements, and so on are all necessary to establish guidelines by which the company will operate and to outline expectations for the various parties.

Many companies start without an operating agreement, but this is not a good idea if you have partners with a financial interest in the business, whether that is your best friend, son, daughter, or other investors. In fact, some states require LLCs (limited liability companies) to have operating agreements in place.

The operating agreement governs the internal operations of the business in a way that suits the needs of the owners; it structures your business's finances and organization, and provides rules and regulations for its operation. The document typically includes percentage of ownership interest, allocation of profits and losses, and members' rights and responsibilities. Be sure to include provisions for issues you think are important: What happens if one of your partners or investors is fired or quits the business – how do you handle his investment? How do you handle a partner's investment if she becomes ill or dies? How do you make the decision if one investor wants to sell and the others do not? These are often tough discussions with the other investors, but it is important to establish firm rules in advance and know that everyone is playing by them. Without such agreements in place, you open yourself up to nasty misunderstandings at the least and costly litigation at the worst.

While there is a great deal of background information in books and online about operating agreements, it is wise to have your attorney draft or review the final agreement. And you certainly should consult your financial advisor before signing any agreement that concerns your income, assets, and liabilities.

Our entrepreneurial client Dan could have saved himself a great deal of pain and financial stress if he had slowed down and assessed carefully his own skill set and the skills necessary to build a start-up health-care technology company. If he had recognized that he was stepping so far outside his sphere of expertise, he could have taken on partners who could help fill the skills gap; and with proper agreements in place, he could also have better shared the financial liabilities among partners.

I should note, however, that taking on partners carries its own complications. While most of us think of a business partnership as chiefly a financial relationship, it is in many ways more like a marriage. The relationship is as emotional as it is financial. And the more partners you include, the more complex the relationships may be, with alliances and animosities forming and shifting over time.

I am so fortunate with the partners I chose 27 years ago. Jim Bruyette and Pete Speros have been with me since the very beginning of SBSB. Our other initial partner, Eleanor Blayney, retired from our company a few years ago. We have had our fair share of arguments and disagreements, but in the end we always trusted and respected one another, just like in a well-tested yet strong marriage.

As with any relationship, your business partnership is most likely to prosper if you agree on clear goals at the outset, define your roles and responsibilities, and communicate effectively, frequently, and with respect.

Beware the High-risk, High-cost Start-up

While every new business carries some risk, certain types of businesses and industries are far more precarious than others. Opening a restaurant, for example, is considered a high-risk business, because it requires a lot of start-up capital, demands a great deal of time and energy, and is dependent upon good location, a winning theme, and often a star chef.

Manufacturing is another area that carries a high level of risk, in part because it requires a large capital investment as well as specialized knowledge of the operations, supply chain, delivery mechanisms, and so on.

A client, Ed, had retired but still had considerable capital and an itch to start a company. Together with several partners, Ed decided to found a company that would manufacture wood and laminate flooring. His partners had a great deal of experience in the industry, and the plan was for Ed to serve as financial backer and CEO while his partners handled manufacturing, operations, marketing, and sales. Other than Ed, none of the group had experience running a company.

Ed's partners were terrific marketing and salespeople; they knew how to talk to people, how to land customers, and how to make their customers happy. Their challenge came in running a manufacturing plant.

Adding to the company's challenges, the flooring business is highly dependent on the economy and the housing market. Any slowdown in housing can dramatically impact success, even if the company is doing well with marketing, sales, and operations.

The 2008 housing crisis hit hard, and so, after several years of hard work and giving it their best, Ed and his partners decided it was time to take their losses and close the business. Running a business can be stressful when your company is doing well; but if the venture is struggling financially, the pressure is a thousand times greater, impacting your work, your health, and your personal life. When starting any business, be mindful of financial and emotional risks that will affect not only you but those around you, including your partner, family, and friends.

Avoid Becoming a Vicarious Entrepreneur

Aiding family is a familiar theme in the realm of entrepreneurship and business start-ups, and perhaps the relationship most often mined is that between parent and child. We have seen this story replicate itself again and again: A parent – often, in the older generations, a father – sees an opportunity to help a child get on his or her feet and is anxious to invest in a business idea the child has.

Our client Ron had enjoyed a successful career as a physician and had saved millions of dollars toward his retirement. He worked late into his 60s and was on track to have a very comfortable retirement, in which any lifestyle he chose was pretty much open to him.

Ron's daughter Amy, meanwhile, started a retail fashion business, and Ron made an early investment. For a while, the company did well and the outlook was promising. It was at this high point, when all was stable, that Ron made what would turn out to be his biggest mistake. Amy, buoyed by the initial success of the start-up, upgraded her lifestyle significantly, buying a house she could not truly afford in an affluent neighborhood. Because Amy couldn't qualify for the second mortgage she needed, Ron cosigned, guaranteeing the mortgage for his daughter.

In the economic downturn of 2008–2009, however, Amy's company, like so many others, suffered dramatic losses. At the same time, the value of real estate plummeted and she was underwater in the house. Though the house was now worth much less than what Amy had paid, the large monthly payment was fixed, and Ron was on the hook because he had cosigned. Settled comfortably in the affluent town where they lived, Amy's family had trouble making needed lifestyle adjustments when income from the business bottomed out, and Ron felt compelled to help out financially. Soon, Ron was bleeding money as he tried to keep the company afloat, keep up with his daughter's mortgage payments, and cushion the financial shock for Amy and her children.

Facing a business's failure can be wrenching, and in Ron's case, the matter was made more complex because it involved his relationship with his daughter. From the time our kids start playing soccer, we as parents sometimes overinvest emotionally (and financially) in our kids' dreams – we may even make their dreams our own. In doing this, we place on them our own hopes and live vicariously as they do the things in life we did not. Ron invested in Amy's company because he believed in his daughter – and that is a good thing – but he also took a lot of pride in having a child who was a successful business owner and who had taken risks that he never had. For this reason, Ron kept propping the company up, even after it was clear to most outsiders that he was throwing good money after bad.

Ron nearly threw away his own lifetime of work to benefit his daughter's dream. Not only did this come close to cratering Ron's financial independence, but it put a strain on the father-daughter relationship.

My partner Jim Bruyette sums up our advisory's philosophy regarding the kind of investments Ron made in his daughter's venture and mortgage: Help your kids, by all means, but *cap your exposure.* Give your children what you can so they can pursue their dreams, and support them emotionally and financially to the extent that you reasonably can, but keep in view the health of your retirement plans. Remember that you have limited time to recover from financial setbacks and, once you've retired, less opportunity to make back the money you've lost in entrepreneurial investments.

Seek Advice

Too often, we financial advisors learn of a new venture or risky investment only after the business was launched or the investment made. (Of course, we also have clients who don't buy an ice cream cone without consulting us, and this is largely a difference between personality types – some folks are naturally cautious while others are more freewheeling or impulsive.)

At the point that they sense they are in real trouble, clients may come to us and say, "Alright, I've got a mess here. What do you suggest?" While the solutions we apply are highly individualized and tailored to the person's financial situation and business challenges, I can share our general approach.

First, we want to understand why the business exists: What is the core purpose of the business? What strong need or desire does the business fulfill for potential customers or clients? Next, we need to determine who is involved in the business and define the key roles and responsibilities of those people. Then, we examine the financial statements and evaluate how close the business is to becoming profitable or shutting down. What are the ramifications if the business closes? Estimate what it would take to save the company – and assess, too, *why* it would be worth saving. If you think the business is worth saving, revisit the Five P's of developing a business plan discussed earlier.

Those who are keen to start companies or invest in new ventures are often people who believe that because they are successful at one thing, they can be successful at everything. We have seen too many people who have made money in one career become overconfident in their ability to make money in another business or investment venture. They forget the hard work that they put into building their career and the luck that was involved in their success. If you think it will be simple to re-create that success, think again!

Starting a business might be the right thing to do, but it is unlikely to be simple or easy. People who want you to invest in their business or sign on as a partner will often play on your ego, complimenting you on how successful you were. The comments are flattering – and possibly well deserved – but you should take them with a grain of salt.

When any client, but especially one who is retired or close to retirement age, comes to us and asks our advice regarding investment in a new business (her own or another's), we certainly want to explore both the opportunity and the downside risk to the assets already accumulated. In such situations, it is helpful to know what you can afford to lose and what you can't. Set a predetermined dollar amount that you define as your retirement nest egg and do not allow your investment in the business to exceed that amount. Period. You don't want your entrepreneurial investment to disrupt your retirement plans, forcing you back into a traditional job to make up any shortfall. And before jumping in, ask yourself whether the stress involved in running a start-up, even a successful one, is worth it at this time in your life.

It's Not All Uphill

We've looked at some of the ways entrepreneurship can lead to a retirement fail, endangering the healthy post-work life for which you've saved for so many years. But the news is not all dire. Even if you think you'd find traditional retirement stultifying, there are many options that can give you greater freedom and flexibility while still offering you some of the rewards that come with challenging work.

Phased Retirement

First, many people today don't simply stop working altogether on some fixed and final retirement date. We are moving away from the era in which long-time employees collected a gold watch for good service to the company and then went home to sit in a rocking chair on the porch or play cards with other retirees, as popular "golden ager" images would have it.

Today, many people contemplate a phased retirement, in which they drop the number of days per week they work, service fewer clients, or generally begin to slow down and divest themselves of many work responsibilities. Depending upon the type of work you do, you may continue working well into your 70s or even into your 80s or later – work that is not dependent on physical strength or endurance can be done as long as health and mental sharpness permit, assuming the industry does not have mandatory retirement requirements.

> According to WorldatWork, an association of human resources managers, approximately 30% of large employers offer some kind of flexible retirement options to their workers, including part-time and job-sharing arrangements.[3]

It's important to note that phased retirement typically brings with it a reduction in salary and benefits, including health insurance and life insurance benefits, so it's important to talk with your financial planner and human resources representative to understand how these cutbacks may impact your overall financial picture.

Low-risk Ventures

Clients sometimes express boredom with life in retirement and go looking for ways to stay engaged with the world. And there's no reason you can't stay active and take on new work challenges, if that's what interests you. I encourage anyone with an entrepreneurial bent to explore areas that are not capital intensive and which can be easily started – or easily dismantled if you don't enjoy the work or if your circumstances should change. Consulting, either compensated or on a pro bono basis, and nonprofit work are both excellent ways to contribute your time and talent on your own terms.

Paul, a client who was itching to keep himself busy after he retired from his work in sales, came to me and floated ideas for a business he was looking into. He was talking about opening a restaurant or a cafe, as he enjoyed good food and also liked the vibrant atmosphere of local coffee joints, but I pushed him to keep thinking about other activities he enjoys. While eateries and coffee shops can enjoy spectacular success, they typically require a lot of capital to start and also demand a great deal of daily attention, as well as experience running an eating establishment.

He continued to brainstorm on his own and we had continuing conversations about his interests and aptitude, as well as his requirements for work in this period of his life. Paul wanted to maintain flexibility in terms of his time commitment and also contribute something of value to his community.

Eventually, Paul, an avid gardener, got onto the board of a nonprofit devoted to the local arboretum. From that board, he was invited to join another. I'd been active in several boards myself, and directed Paul to some resources that would help him make the most of his experience. He immersed himself in the details of what it takes to be a successful board member and ultimately got certified as a trainer for members of nonprofit boards.

As a star salesperson, Paul had learned what motivates people and he understands how people make decisions, insight that was invaluable in the nonprofit arena. He had the right skill set and he loves teaching; in addition, the work required little in the way of start-up costs and could be aligned with the more relaxed lifestyle he sought in (semi)retirement. Consulting and other businesses that sell services are relatively low risk, as they require sweat equity but not much capital. Paul is now making six figures as a consultant, teaching nonprofit board members how to be more effective in their work – and, as importantly, he finds his work fulfilling and well suited to the kind of life he wants to lead in his later years.

Paul's new career gave him something that is important to a satisfying life in retirement: A sense of identity. Finding your identity in your post-work years can be more challenging than most acknowledge. Don't underestimate your need to have something fulfilling to do, or an organization or community to belong to, that keeps you engaged in life and makes you feel good about getting up every morning.

Finding Work You Love

The most attractive postretirement work takes advantage of your skills and your experience and, not least, is something you truly enjoy doing. Think about what fascinates you and what you are good at. Look for activities – either compensated or volunteer – that call on the same skills you excelled at in your job, even though you may be operating in a different arena. Paul, for example, was a terrific salesperson, and his dynamic personality and people skills translated well to teaching and training.

Unless you are working specifically to increase your income, don't overlook uncompensated opportunities. Even when you begin as a volunteer, you may gain valuable contacts and experience that you can later leverage to create a business opportunity.

Look at the type of environment that allows you to give back and to share your expertise. By the time you hit retirement age, you've had 30, 40, or 50 years of experience that other people can benefit from, and you get the intangible reward of passing your wisdom to a new generation. People who love their work are those who find meaning in what they are doing. So identify the impact you want to make in the world and look for a way to move toward that goal.

Retirement is a time that you can afford to put your energies toward your life's purpose, and if the work of your career didn't fulfill you, this is your opportunity. There are many ways to do this, even without setting off on a full-fledged entrepreneurial adventure. And if you've determined that a business start-up is indeed what you want to do, enter the endeavor fully prepared. Entrepreneurship becomes a retirement fail only when you lack the necessary skills or spirit, launch without adequate plans in place, and neglect to limit your exposure to the risks. Equipped with a solid understanding of the perils and the possibilities, you are primed to succeed in whatever work venture you choose.

Tips for Entrepreneurs

Based on my experience and insight of 30-plus years running a business and working with owners of both start-ups and thriving companies, there are four critical tasks you need to execute well if you are to become a successful entrepreneur:

- Build a business plan focusing on the 5 P's (Purpose, People, Process, Pricing, and Profits).

(continued)

(Continued)

- Create a culture that embraces your values as well as those of your employees, your clients, and your investors.
- Develop a firm strategy around growth, management, and productivity.
- Have fun! You, your employees, and your clients should love working together and should enjoy being in one another's company.

CHAPTER 6

Swindler's Mark

One morning you open up your e-mail and see a message from your real estate lawyer regarding a property you are looking to buy. It's good news; the sale is proceeding, and you just need to wire a payment to the bank as instructed. You go ahead and wire the amount – a little more than $1 million – and though your bank stops the payment temporarily, you give your verbal okay for the transfer to proceed. All seems well, until you learn that your attorney did not send you any such e-mail. When you contact the US bank to which you wired your payment, you find out that the account has been cleared out – your money has been sent to an account in Hong Kong.

You may think that this sort of thing happens to people who are unsophisticated, out of touch, or unaware of the prevalence of financial scams – but the scenario outlined above actually happened in 2017 to a New York State Supreme Court judge in her early 50s.[1] While we often picture the victims of phishing scams to be uneducated, naïve, or even beginning to be forgetful or inattentive to details – and, certainly, people who fit that profile are particularly vulnerable to scams – they're not the only ones who can be taken in. The incidence of financial fraud is rising dramatically and, aided by technology, the scams are becoming increasingly sophisticated.

In 2016, $16 billion was scammed from 15.4 million US victims of identity fraud, according to the *2017 Identity Fraud Study* conducted by Javelin Strategy & Research. That victim count represents a 16% increase over the previous year.[2]

Targets of Financial Schemes

While the incidence of fraud is rising across all generations (and, according to one recent report, may be particularly high for Millennials[3]), exploitation of older Americans is reaching epidemic proportions, described by MetLife as the "Crime of the 21st Century." Just how much money is being swindled from seniors is a huge question mark: A MetLife estimate gauged the number to be about $3 billion annually,[4] but an estimate from financial services firm True Link puts the costs 12 times higher, at more than $36 billion.[5]

The diversity of estimates reflects the fact that there is no standard definition of what financial fraud and exploitation encompass as well as the differing methodologies used to collect and extrapolate from the data. Whatever number you choose to believe, the costs are inarguably in the billions annually, so clearly financial fraud is a massive threat for those approaching retirement or in their retirement years.

One reason that swindlers target people who are well into their careers or in retirement is that this demographic typically has a sizable nest egg that can be tapped. In addition, people in older age categories are more likely to own their homes and to have good credit, which makes them attractive to fraudsters. Those in older generations may also have been trained to be polite to strangers and often find it harder to disengage quickly from unsolicited phone calls or unscrupulous salespeople.

Another reason that scammers target older Americans is that they are less likely to report fraud, often fearing that they may be thought unable to handle their financial affairs. They may feel embarrassed at having been taken in by the scam and unsure of where to report this type of crime. Whether you are a victim of fraud or whether it is your parent or other family member who has been the target, it's important to report instances of fraud as well as attempts to gain access to your personal accounts so that authorities can track patterns, warn potential victims, and prosecute offenders; the Resources section lists agencies to which you can report fraud.

Schemes to defraud range from those that seem obvious to most of us – we wonder who still believes that a Nigerian prince needs our help to access his funds (this scam has been circulating since the 1970s, after all) – to complex and targeted traps like the one that caught the New York judge.

Small-scale fraudsters may siphon off relatively modest amounts of cash from lots of victims, but there are also more sophisticated schemes that promote "investment opportunities" that are either inappropriate for the individual or are complete swindles, failing to deliver anything remotely like the product offered. These can total tens of thousands, or even hundreds of thousands, of dollars in losses for a single victim. Watch the TV show *American Greed* and you will hear numerous stories of people who seem perfectly nice and might even be part of your neighborhood or church but are working their magic. These con artists get unsuspecting people to trust them, then make very healthy and consistent rates of return on their "investment."

A 2015 True Link Financial study estimated that nearly $17 billion was taken via tactics that are technically legal but are specifically designed to confuse and mislead older people.[6] Sadly, the perpetrator of financial abuse is all too often a family member who is experiencing financial difficulties.

Bigger Targets, Bigger Scams

The largest and best-known financial fraud, and the one that serves as a cautionary tale for investors across the globe, is, of course, Bernie Madoff's $65 billion Ponzi scheme, which unraveled in 2008 after he confessed the fraud to his two sons. More than 63,000 claims were filed against Madoff,[7] and among his investors were banks, hedge funds, charities, foundations, endowments, and such high-profile figures as writer and activist Elie Wiesel, actors Kevin Bacon and Kyra Sedgwick, the family of former governor Eliot Spitzer, and Mets owner Fred Wilpon.

While operations on such a large scale are rare, they do happen, and there are many instances of smaller schemes that don't make headline news. In a Ponzi scheme, the operator generates revenue for earlier investors from money paid in by new investors rather than through legitimate business activities. The scheme crumbles when there are not enough new investors to pay out the purported returns or when a large number of investors ask to cash out.

Ponzi schemes are closely related to pyramid schemes, but in a classic pyramid scheme participants are involved in recruiting additional distributors for a product (which may not exist), and the collapse is typically quick as the number of new investors required to keep the scheme going grows exponentially. A Ponzi scheme, in which the investor need only hand over cash, can go on for quite some time, particularly if participants reinvest their money rather than taking returns. Madoff's scheme likely began somewhere around 2001 and continued until the end of 2008, when the down market put increasing pressure on the operation.

Madoff was able to keep the scheme going for so long because he controlled the paperwork; he generated false statements that showed outsize returns to his clients. As long as most investors stayed with the investment and as long as new money flowed in, he was able to keep the fraud afloat.

Ponzi schemes are sometimes discovered when a potential investor (or an investigator from a government agency) starts digging deep and finds out it's a Wizard of Oz scenario, just a little man behind a curtain pulling levers and not the big wizard he expected. When somebody gets too close and starts asking too many questions, the fraudster will often say, "We are closed to new investors," putting the potential troublemaker at bay.

Madoff actually used exclusivity not only to ward off those who asked too many questions but also to create a buzz about the investments. He'd tell those who wanted to invest that the firm was only taking limited funds and he would have to get back to them. He and other scammers create a sense of rare opportunity that investors must jump at or lose out. "The window is only going to open briefly," they warn prospects. "I know you were thinking about putting in $100,000, but the window is only going to open for a short time so maybe you want to invest $200,000 or $300,000." And the potential client thinks, "I'd better do $300,000." He feels lucky to get in.

Real Estate Rackets

One scheme I sometimes see clients become interested in is real estate investment schemes or investment property clubs. There are some such arrangements that operate in an aboveboard manner, though they are inherently risky. Others are legal but wildly overstate possible gains and do not represent a solid investment, and your money is tied up for many years in a no- or low-return environment; still other real estate schemes operate on the margins of the law or even completely fraudulently, depending upon the representations made.

In many real estate investments or property clubs, the investor puts in money with the promise of high interest on the capital invested or a sizable increase in the property's value, resulting in large gains. Any time you're told that your return is guaranteed to be 8 or 9% percent or higher, you should be wary. The person running the venture invests half the capital in property and uses the other half to pay "returns" to the investors; however, investors are actually being paid back out of their own money.

While the person running the investment or property club is collecting significant fees, he expresses tremendous optimism that the investment property will indeed yield a nice return when sold at the end of the investment period, but it is unlikely that the ultimate payout will match the promises made. Investors initially feel good because they are getting regular checks, which they assume is a return on their investment rather than a return of their investment capital. Most investors have a comfort level with real estate because of its strong history of appreciation in decades past, but it's highly unlikely that they will get a decent return and may even lose money, especially when fees are taken into account.

It can be extremely difficult for someone who is not well informed about real estate accounting to spot red flags in such property investments – in order to see the failings in the plan, you would need to have a strong grasp of what real estate investment documents should say and the analysis that should be provided.

Stop and consider whether you have the right knowledge and insight to make this type of investment decision on your own. Before investing in any of these offerings, I recommend that you have your financial advisor review the documentation, talk to the general partners, and provide some financial analysis on how the properties may perform during different investment periods. Besides outright fraud, outlandish fees, mismanagement, and questionable valuations are often the killers in these types of investments. Be sure to scrutinize the investment up front, or you will likely be stuck with a poor investment for a long time.

Annuities and Inappropriate Financial Products

People of any age can be taken in by high-pressure sales tactics, and unethical agents prey on prospects' fears of an unstable market or push financial products that are lucrative for the agent but unsuitable for the client. While many of the activities in this arena may be perfectly legal, they may still take advantage of a client's misapprehensions of what he is buying. When financial products are deceptively marketed or when the true costs are not disclosed, the activity may cross over and enter fraud territory.

Older or ill people can be particularly susceptible, because an agent may be able to capitalize on their shorter time horizon. In some cases, agents persuade older retirees to buy annuities that tie up money for a decade or longer and structure the contract so that cash left in the annuity remains with the company rather than passing to beneficiaries after the person dies. It would be a pretty unusual situation in which it makes sense for an 80-year-old widow to be buying an annuity, yet we see it happen.

Life insurance and annuities may also be exchanged for a new policy either with another company or with the same company, in practices known as "twisting" and "churning," respectively. The agent represents the new policy as having greater value, though in reality you have added surrender fees and commissions that make the exchange costly for the policyholder but rewarding for the agent. Changing policies may in fact be a good idea, but any update to an annuity or life insurance policy should benefit the client rather than the agent. If an agent is recommending you change your insurance policy or annuity plan, ask if he is being paid a commission on the trade. If he is, seek out a second opinion by another independent agent or a Certified Financial Planner™ (CFP®) professional who is qualified to review the policy, and ask if you should purchase or exchange the policy.

Annuities may be an appropriate investment for you but they represent a major financial commitment, and you should be sure you understand all the terms of the contract and that you are working with a reputable, licensed agent or advisor who is following all applicable state laws. Don't succumb to sales pitches that push deals offered "only today" or promise special signing bonuses.

Be aware that agents who represent themselves as financial consultants may in fact have no financial background, and they may push complex contracts that are difficult to understand or that have high annual fees or surrender charges. Reports from ratings agencies such as Moody's, Standard & Poor's, and Fitch can help you evaluate the history of the company you are considering working with, but it's best to have a trusted, independent financial advisor and/or tax professional review any financial product you are considering purchasing. These professionals can not only assess the financial soundness of the product, they can evaluate liquidity issues, suitability, and tax implications for your particular situation.

Phishing, Phone Scams, and Identity Theft

Clicking on a suspect link, giving personal information to a caller, or using your debit or credit card at the wrong outlet – any of these things can lead to fraudulent charges, account takeovers, new accounts opened in your name, and a host of other very bad things. Some of the operations are cleverly designed to confuse even tech-savvy people, while others may seem crude but nevertheless net unwary victims.

My mom, in fact, faced two approaches within just a couple of weeks. She received a phone call one afternoon from a Florida number, and it was young man who, in a shaking voice, said, "Grandma? I'm so glad you're home, I really need your help." She said, "Will? Is that you?" And the young man replied, "Yes, it's me, Will."

He went on to tell my mom that he'd been in an accident and needed $2,500 immediately. Understandably worried for her grandson and wanting to help, she agreed, and was getting details about where to send the money when my sister intervened. My sister, who happened to be visiting, took the phone and began asking questions, at which point the man hung up.

This guy, preying on the concern of a worried grandmother, had only to offer the barest suggestion before she supplied him with a name he could claim and use to manipulate her. But even if she had not stepped in and provided a name, some criminals do their homework and know enough personal details about their target to make their story convincing.

Later that week, Mom began receiving calls from the "IRS." People tend to panic when the IRS contacts them, and these fraudulent calls can be aggressive, threatening arrest, revocation of drivers' licenses, and deportation, all in an attempt to get you to make an immediate payment. The callers spoof numbers to make it appear on your caller ID that it is the IRS calling, and they may have details such as your name, address, and other personal information.

According to the IRS, more than five thousand victims have paid out $26.5 million to such scammers. Be aware that the IRS will never demand immediate payment of a tax bill over the phone, and will not call regarding unpaid taxes without having first mailed a bill. You are also entitled to an appeal process. All this is to say that any call you receive claiming to be from the IRS is very likely to be fraudulent. If you receive such a call, hang up immediately and report the call to the IRS.

My mom, luckily, knows that I handle all major financial matters for the family, so she was not tempted to make that urgent payment without consulting me. It's a good general practice to tell any such caller that you will refer the matter to your attorney or financial advisor to resolve – that usually results in a hang-up.

A client of mine was also faced with a scammer approaching his mother, but the outcome was not as good. In this case, the fraud was a lottery scam, and there was a lengthy correspondence that accompanied the fraud. The woman, who was elderly, received a phone call indicating that she had won the lottery, but that taxes were due before the prize could be paid out. According to the nice man on the phone, the taxes on the million-dollar lottery prize amounted to $250,000, but it did not have to be paid all at once; the man told her they could arrange installments. This sweet-talking guy painted an appealing picture of how a million dollars could change her life and the lives of her children, and she was swayed by his charm and his concern for her family.

Though her son explained the scam and told her she would not receive any prize money, she still felt compelled to make the "payments" as bills from the scammer arrived via e-mail. After she made a few payments to the scammers, her family stepped in and became more involved in her day-to-day finances.

Scammers rely on things people want – a more secure future, a windfall that will help them or their kids – and things they fear – a child or grandchild in distress, trouble with the IRS – to get victims to act quickly and without questioning. Know that there is no legitimate request that can be made where you cannot call the person back at a number that you can look up and verify independently. Never give personal information to an unknown caller who initiates the call.

Financial Exploitation by Family or Friends

Financial exploitation is a category of abuse in which vulnerable older adults, or sometimes those with disabilities, are deprived of their assets, often by a person close to them such as a family member, caregiver, friend, neighbor, or trusted professional. Financial mistreatment ranges from outright stealing of funds or property to coercing a person to sign a contract or other document that he normally would not sign. Instances of financial exploitation are sometimes complicated by other types of elder abuse, such as physical or emotional abuse or neglect.

Financial exploitation is vastly underreported. The National Adult Protective Services Association estimates that only one in 44 cases of financial abuse is reported; 90% of abusers are family members or trusted others.[8]

Financial exploitation tends to be most problematic for elderly or ill adults, who may no longer have the ability to make sound decisions; they may be losing some cognitive capacity, be isolated, be fearful of the abuser or ashamed of the abuse, or a combination of these.

An unscrupulous family member may use a power of attorney granted by the victim to steal money from accounts for his or her own benefit. If bank accounts are set up jointly, to allow the family member to easily pay the older person's bills or perform banking tasks, he may siphon money out of the account, or he may cash stolen checks or make withdrawals using an ATM card. Among the most heartbreaking cases are those in which a family member threatens the elderly person or denies him or her necessities or medical care in order to preserve the person's assets for his own use.

While the vast majority of hired caregivers such as home health aides or in-home nurses are people of integrity doing difficult work, some may exploit a person under their care. Among the common ways that care providers take advantage of their clients are falsifying time sheets, charging for services not performed, paying their own bills using the client's funds, removing cash or valuables from the client's home, or pocketing change from shopping trips or other errands.

If you have a loved one you consider vulnerable, pay attention to warning signs that may indicate he is being taken advantage of, such as significant withdrawals from accounts or unexpected changes to the person's insurance policies, titles, or will. Note and question instances in which a person who was previously on top of his financial matters no longer seems to manage them well; he may be experiencing lessening capacity, or it's possible that someone else has gained access to his accounts.

When practicable, involve several family members in care and decision making; for example, if all the siblings in the family are reviewing mom's bank accounts periodically, it is more difficult for one of the children or another person to misuse funds. Make sure the person you are concerned about feels that she can talk to you about anything that worries her; ask a lot of questions of anyone living in the home or spending a great deal of time with the older person, as well as of any caregivers or other companions she may have.

If you suspect financial exploitation, confront the suspected abuser with your misgivings and report any theft to law enforcement. Local social service agencies can also be good resources for aid to victims of financial abuse.

Protecting Yourself

Fortunately, though financial fraud of various types is widespread and growing, there are some simple steps that you can take to prevent yourself from becoming a victim of financial fraud.

Identity Theft and Credit Card Fraud

- If a representative from an institution or a firm you deal with – your bank or your insurance company, for instance – calls and requests personal information, make sure to do a call-back. Locate an independently verifiable telephone number and place the call yourself.
- Never act based on an e-mail; if you are contacted by e-mail, make a call to the person using an independently verifiable telephone number and confirm instructions verbally. The same is true of postal mail. Call the person who sent the inquiry to make certain that the request is legitimate.
- Do not use your e-mail address as your user name, and use different user names for your online credit card, bank, and investment accounts.
- Do not click on computer links from people you do not know or that appear suspicious. If the e-mail was sent by someone you know and you have doubts about links it contains, contact

the person. Clicking on malicious links may lead to files that download additional malware onto compromised computers, including info stealers, which can gather log-in credentials for online banking accounts, social media, and other online accounts.

- Don't use easy-to-guess passwords for bank and credit card accounts, such as a pet's name or the name of a spouse or child. Don't use one password for several different accounts; if one is compromised by a breach, the accounts that share that password will also be vulnerable.
- For important online accounts, particularly bank accounts, set up dual authentication, so you can't get into the account based on user name and password alone. Dual authentication requires that the institution send a temporary code that you must input or that you answer a security question. It is far too easy for hackers to access accounts with user name and password.
- While it is far more difficult to steal securities than cash, you can also set up dual authentication for most brokerage accounts.
- Beware of skimmers. These are malicious card readers that collect data from the magnetic strip on your debit or credit card. Check for obvious signs of tampering at ATMs and card readers. Shield your personal identification number (PIN) as you input it; this will prevent fraud if the thief is relying on a camera to capture your PIN, though it will not help if a PIN overlay has been installed on the keyboard.
- Debit cards are essentially cash. For this reason, I suggest limiting your use of debit cards. Maintain a small balance if you do use one, and be careful of the venues where you swipe – gas station pumps are notorious for housing skimmers that can steal your data. The best security would be to change your debit card every six months, but that is burdensome so most people don't do it.
- Review your debit and credit card accounts frequently and report any suspicious activity in a timely way. If you report theft to your bank or credit card issuer right away, you should not be held liable for the loss.
- Sign new credit cards as soon as they arrive and destroy old or expired cards by cutting them up or shredding them.

Also, shred all unused preapproved credit applications and any other mail or documents that contain personal details.

- Consider freezing your credit with all credit agencies (Equifax, TransUnion, and Experian). There are inconveniences (and costs) as well as benefits to freezing your credit, however, so this approach may not be appropriate for everyone. While this move can thwart attempts by thieves trying to open new accounts in your name, it also means that you will need to take steps if you want to open an account, apply for a mortgage or car loan, or rent an apartment, for example, and it does not prevent theft from existing accounts.
- Consider enrolling with an identity protection service such as LifeLock or Identity Guard.

Ponzi Schemes and Investment Fraud

- Do your own due diligence or hire an experienced, independent financial advisor such as a CFP® professional. This is the most critical piece of advice I can give. Investors often don't do the analysis they ought to. They buy into an idea because their brother-in-law or their attorney or the deacon at their church is in this particular investment; those friends say, "Warren Buffet is investing in this." So you think, "Warren Buffet is a smart guy, he knows about investing, it must be good." Don't just follow the crowd and assume that others have already done the due diligence. Research the firm and the investment yourself, and turn to third-party reviewers to assure the investment is sound.
- Do not hire a financial advisor or money manager who takes custody of your assets; that is how Bernie Madoff's scam was able to last so long. Your best protection is to work with independent advisors who use third-party custodians such as Schwab, Pershing, Fidelity, Vanguard, TD Ameritrade, or another reputable custodian. The third-party custodian provides an independent listing and pricing of your assets every day.
- Be wary of outsize returns that don't make sense. Returns that are consistently high every quarter, even in a down market, can indicate that statements are falsified. Market volatility is normal.

- Look carefully at documentation. Do reports and other documents undergo scrutiny by someone other than the person putting them out? Most mutual funds are subject to a Securities and Exchange Commission (SEC) filing, so the information is available and third-party companies such as Morningstar go through those filings and compile reports, which you can access. On the private equity side, the key is to get an independent review by a financial advisor who knows how to evaluate the investment. It is worth paying someone with expertise to render an opinion, as most people are not skilled in evaluating these types of investments. In summary, don't make an investment based on a friend, neighbor, your lawyer, and so on, and do not rely on an evaluation by anyone affiliated with the company selling the investment, even if that person is purported to be an expert.

Listen to Your Doubts

Everyone wants enormous returns with little to no risk, but unfortunately that's not possible. Any financial advisor managing stocks, bonds, or other investments will have some variability year over year. If you are guaranteed giant gains with little or no downside risk or hear of an investment that sounds too good to be true, it probably is. As P. T. Barnum said, "There's a sucker born every minute." But you don't have to be one of them.

Protect Yourself from Scammers

- Advisors and agents offering quick returns and special access are red flags. Legitimate investment professionals do not guarantee outsize returns. Many con artists play up exclusivity or solicit based on relationships and shared affiliations.

- Protect your assets by monitoring your investments and asking questions. Choose an advisor that uses a third-party custodian and make certain you are receiving written reports from the custodian as well as from your advisor. Review the reports and question anything that seems out of the ordinary, such as large, unauthorized transfers.

(continued)

(*Continued*)

- Don't feel pressured to make a decision quickly. Take time and do your due diligence; as a starting point, you can check the Financial Industry Regulatory Authority (FINRA) and the SEC sites for information.

- Scammers take advantage of people's tendency to be polite. Don't be a "courtesy victim."

- Do not act on e-mail solicitations.

- Report investment fraud or abuse (see Resources). Investors who have been victims of financial fraud are often embarrassed, but don't let injured pride prevent you from informing the proper authorities.

CHAPTER 7

Health Matters

However you picture your life in retirement – whether you want to take up watercolor painting at last, travel through Tuscany with your spouse, or give back by volunteering in your community – your plans depend upon a certain level of health and energy. If you've always been blessed with a sturdy constitution, you like to think you'll continue that way. And if you are lucky, you will simply close your eyes one night far, far in the future – when you are, say, 105 – and pass away peacefully in your sleep.

But what if that's not how it happens? What if a health crisis disrupts your retirement plans? Are you prepared for the effects that a sudden heart attack, a cancer diagnosis, a stroke, or the onset of dementia may have on you and your family?

Perhaps we can never truly be prepared for any of these things, but it is worth giving them some thought and putting in place the contingency plans we can, without tipping over into obsessing about a future that may never materialize. And it also benefits us greatly to do what we can to stay as healthy as possible. While we can't control all disease and decline, there's a lot we *can* do to maintain and enhance our health as we age.

My work as a financial advisor concerns chiefly my clients' investment portfolio and financial health, but I also know that the big picture is critical. Every aspect of life – financial, relationship, work, happiness, health – is related to every other aspect, and your physical, mental, and emotional health have an enormous impact on your ability to enjoy retirement and remain financially fit as you age.

Retirement, Interrupted

When I talk about health matters as a retirement disruptor, I'm not talking primarily about bankrupting yourself as a result of a medical condition. That can happen, certainly, and it's critical to protect yourself by carrying adequate medical coverage and adjusting financial plans in the event of a serious diagnosis, but I'm referring in part to the lost potential to enjoy the retirement you desire – for you and, possibly, for your spouse.

Unfortunately, life sometimes throws us curveballs and we have to do our best to adjust. Sometimes couples plan to travel extensively in retirement or to live at a golf resort and enjoy their time together. But a person whose activity level becomes severely curtailed by health problems will need to alter his or her expectations for what life will be like. And when one spouse faces a health crisis and ends up in a nursing home or passes away prematurely, the other can feel bereft, their vision for years of happy retirement with their spouse forever changed. Over the years I have seen how the "healthy" spouse, the one without Alzheimer's or stroke, who is often providing full- or part-time care for their spouse, is impacted emotionally and physically. When health issues arise, it is challenging for the entire family.

My dad retired at 60 and later suffered a sudden fatal heart attack, passing away at 71. My mother, only 67 at the time, has had 19 years without my father. She is fine financially, and she loves spending time with her children and grandchildren, but she missed the retirement lifestyle that she and my dad had planned together. It is hard to lose a longtime spouse, even when you are healthy and have a loving family around you.

An adverse health event is an interruption to your retirement that you don't have full control over, unfortunately; if you or your spouse are confronted with catastrophic illness, your retirement is going to be affected. The best thing you can do is be prepared with contingencies so that you can be supported – financially, physically, and emotionally. Realizing that there's not always going to be an unambiguously rosy outcome, what do you need to know?

In 2015, the 10 leading causes of death were heart disease, cancer, chronic lower respiratory diseases, unintentional injuries, stroke, Alzheimer's disease, diabetes, influenza and pneumonia, kidney disease, and suicide. These 10 causes accounted for 74% of the 2.7 million deaths in 2015.[1]

Refining Your Views on Health Care

It's a good idea to take stock of your values, your goals, and your general attitude toward medical care before you must make critical decisions about health-care needs. Having a firm idea of your philosophy and communicating it to others can simplify decision making down the line and help you lead the kind of life you want as you age.

As you get older, you are more likely to develop health problems that aren't necessarily "cured" by a doctor's visit and instead require ongoing management – high blood pressure, arthritis, diabetes, high cholesterol. Conditions like these mean that your visits to doctors and other health-care providers will be more regular – health care becomes part of your routine rather than something you worry about only when there's an urgent problem.

And as you get older, the urgent problems may be more urgent than they were when you were younger. A little later in the chapter I'll talk about advance directives and the paperwork you need in place. In preparation for your conversations with family and health-care providers about your wishes, think about the type of medical care you normally seek and what you want to receive as you age.

There is a vast continuum of medical intervention, and people feel differently about how much they want to engage with the health-care system. Are you a person who immediately makes a doctor's appointment for a minor cough, or do you tend to wait out your symptoms for a while, hoping any illness will resolve on its own? Do you prefer to undergo intensive medical testing to make sure any possible issues are uncovered? Would you expect a high level of intervention if you should get sick?

There are no right answers and, whether you are a minimalist or prefer to go all-out when it comes to interventions, the exercise is about understanding the type of care you want to receive. Knowing your own mind, communicating your thoughts to your loved ones, and having a team of health-care providers who understand and respect your approach to care prepares you for health challenges that arise and helps your family make appropriate decisions on your behalf if need be.

Health Insurance

Quality health insurance is a necessity. Today, innovative treatments are curing diseases and turning once life-threatening illnesses into conditions that can be managed, but these advances come at a high price. Health crises and chronic medical problems can eat into retirement savings at an alarming rate if a person is not adequately insured, and health-care needs in retirement represent an enormous wild card.

The clients I work with, who have amassed some wealth and have saved amply for retirement, tend to have excellent health insurance in place. Some have insurance provided by an employer (or former employer, if the person is retired), while others have individual policies or group insurance through a membership they hold. Medicare – the federal health insurance program for people who are 65 or older (and for younger people with disabilities) – can interact with employer-provided or other group insurance once an individual turns 65, so it's important to understand the provisions of your particular plan; for example, some employers' plans transition those who turn 65 to a Medicare plan. Because the insurance landscape is complicated, consult with an advisor who can guide you to the best decisions for you and your family.

While everyone who is eligible to receive Social Security benefits is entitled to Medicare Part A (hospital insurance) and Medicare Part B (medical insurance) when he or she turns 65, some are enrolled automatically (if they are receiving Social Security benefits at least four months before turning 65) while most will need to sign up for these benefits. Most individuals should sign up for Part A but may reject Medicare Part B (which requires a premium) if they wish, in favor of private insurance. Those with higher incomes who do opt for Medicare pay larger premiums than lower-income seniors, and these premiums have been rising over the past several years. Private supplemental insurance can cover out-of-pocket expenses incurred with Medicare, such as copays and hospital deductibles.

I spoke with Jon Katz, principal and founder of Virginia Medical Plans/Katz Insurance Group, about the major missteps he sees his clients make. One of the biggest mistakes, he says, is people's failure to transition to Medicare within the necessary enrollment period. If you are retired at 65, it's fairly clear that you should enroll in Medicare when you turn 65 (and you will be automatically enrolled if you are eligible and are already receiving Social Security benefits). But more and more people are working into their late 60s or 70s, delaying their Social Security benefits, and for them the picture is a little more complicated.

When you leave employment, you have eight months to enroll in Medicare (assuming you are 65 or older and had eligible group insurance through your employer); however, many people choose COBRA (Consolidated Omnibus Budget Reconciliation Act), which allows you to extend coverage by your company's group health insurance at your own expense and continues for 18 months. Jon tells me, "People call me and say, 'I'm in my 17th month of COBRA so now I need to switch to Medicare.' I have to break it to them that there's no way to do that immediately and that they may end up paying a sizable penalty for the rest of their lives."

If you have COBRA and enroll in Medicare, your COBRA may terminate; if you are already enrolled in Medicare when you become eligible for COBRA, however, you must be allowed to enroll in COBRA in addition, under current coordination of benefits rules. Check with your health insurance agent and/or your employer's human resources department to be sure you are enrolling in the appropriate plan within the proper time period.

Because COBRA, even if identical to the company's plan, does not typically qualify as group health coverage from an active employer under Medicare's definitions, failure to sign up for Part B at the appropriate time means that you must wait until the general enrollment period (January 1 to March 31) and your coverage will not begin until July 1 of that year.

Most people who don't enroll in a Medicare plan on time will need to secure a bridge health insurance plan to cover the gap, and this is not always easy to do, depending upon your health history and where you live. Such plans typically exclude preexisting conditions and you can even be denied altogether. When you do receive Medicare Part B, you will also likely be subject to a late-enrollment penalty, which amounts to 10% for every 12-month period that you could have had Part B but did not enroll – and this premium penalty continues for the entire time you are on Part B.

Jon notes that the other issue that catches clients unaware is the decision between a Medicare Advantage Plan (Part C) and Original Medicare (Parts A and B), often augmented with supplemental insurance. In almost every instance, Katz recommends traditional Medicare Parts A and B with supplemental insurance, including Part D (prescription drug coverage); while Medicare Advantage typically features lower premiums, Jon sees this as a false economy. The Medicare Advantage plan is less flexible because you must choose providers from a more limited network, and it can be difficult or impossible to switch plans later if you find yourself dissatisfied. In addition, there may be gaps in coverage in Medicare Advantage plans, yet in many areas supplemental plans are not available.

One of Jon's clients was injured severely in an accident and felt he was getting substandard care from his plan's in-network providers. However, his existing medical problems meant that he would have been denied a Medicare Supplement Plan. The only way he could have avoided undergoing medical underwriting would have been if (1) he moved to a new state or (2) the insurance company pulled the product off the market. Sadly, Jon says, clients call him in tears, frustrated with the care they are receiving yet unable to change to a new provider because of restrictive in-plan networks.

One additional note in the discussion of health insurance regards coverage for your older children. While the Patient Protection and Affordable Care Act (ACA) includes a provision that allows kids to stay on their parents' insurance plans until they are 26, kids who age out without being able to easily afford their own health insurance may opt not to purchase insurance. Unfortunately, one tragic accident or devastating diagnosis can turn that into a disastrous decision.

As a parent, your inclination would be to step in and make sure your ill or injured child receives the best care possible. That is a natural reaction, and I don't know any mom or dad who would not do the same. But, depending upon the size of your nest egg, that event could severely impact your family's finances.

Talk with your adult children about their level of coverage, and if they are lacking health insurance and you are in a position to subsidize them, consider helping them with premiums. That way, if some unforeseen health emergency should occur, your child will have medical coverage and you will be able to focus solely on helping your child get well.

Long-term Care

Long-term care insurance helps pay for services that are generally not covered by health insurance or Medicare because they are not strictly medical care. This type of care typically includes assistance with dressing, bathing, walking, eating, and other activities of daily living. Long-term care (sometimes shortened to LTC) aims to help people suffering from cognitive impairment, chronic illness, or disability maintain the greatest degree of independence possible as they live with their condition, while short-term care such as hospitalization or rehabilitation has recovery as the goal. (We will discuss disability insurance, which helps replace lost income for those who can no longer work, in Chapter 8, "Life's Unpredictabilities.")

Between 1975 and 2015, life expectancy at birth increased from 72.6 to 78.8 years for the total US population. For males, life expectancy increased from 68.8 years in 1975 to 76.3 years in 2015, and for females, life expectancy increased from 76.6 years in 1975 to 81.2 years in 2015.[2]

When people think of long-term care, they usually picture a nursing home, and that is indeed one part of the LTC equation. However, long-term care may also include home care, assisted living, day care, respite care, or care in an Alzheimer's facility. The majority of long-term care is actually performed by family members or friends, but paid caregivers may supplement or supplant care given by family – and as a person becomes more frail or cognitively impaired, the need for care may grow. The cost of services, when they must be paid for, varies widely depending upon the precise services needed, the setting in which they are performed, and the region of the country.

Long-term care insurance policies reimburse policyholders for the cost of caregiving associated with tasks of daily living. When buying long-term care insurance, you can choose from a range of benefits, and the cost of premiums depends upon a number of factors, including your age when you buy the policy, the time period the policy covers (maximum days/years of benefits), the maximum the insurer will pay, the period that must elapse between qualifying for care and the start of benefits (called the elimination period), and the optional benefits you select. Because there are so many available options – including forgoing LTC insurance and paying for the cost of care out of pocket – customizing a plan to your needs is a complex undertaking; consult with your financial advisor and/or a licensed insurance broker for help navigating your choices.

In addition, know that those who are older or in poor health may not qualify for long-term care insurance; the average age of a person who buys LTC coverage is 60, though the average age of a person who purchases a policy through an employer is 50.[3] The cost of long-term care insurance has been rising dramatically in recent years and is likely to increase given the aging US population. Be aware, too, that your premium may increase over time (although some policies offer inflation protection), so check the insurer's history of rate hikes before purchasing a policy.

> According to the US Department of Health and Human Services, nearly 70% of Americans turning 65 today will require some type of long-term care services during their remaining years.[4]

Long-term care insurance is not a necessity for everyone, and no approach is one-size-fits-all. When I talk with clients about long-term care, we look not only at their financial picture – assets plus income – but also at their family health history.

In my family, for instance, the men don't tend to live very long. We don't have Alzheimer's disease in our family, but there's a history of fatal heart attacks. In looking at an LTC plan for one of my male relatives, a five-year policy would probably be appropriate. I might make a different recommendation for a family that had longevity and Alzheimer's as part of their history because people who have Alzheimer's or another form of dementia can require care for 10 or 15 years or more, though that may be changing.

Recently, I was on a plane to San Francisco and I started talking with the man next to me. We got onto the subject of the elderly and Alzheimer's disease, and he was telling me that there is some groundbreaking research showing ways to prevent and even reverse this terrible disease. I was fascinated by the conversation, and so I asked about the research, only to find that I was sitting next to Dr. Dale Bredesen, author of the *New York Times* best seller *The End of Alzheimer's*. What a treat, and it was so inspiring to learn that medical research is finding solutions and cures for Alzheimer's and many other diseases that deprive people of healthy years in retirement. If you have Alzheimer's in your family, I highly recommend Dr. Bredesen's book.

Until medical researchers find effective therapies for all age-related illnesses, though, we will have to deal with the reality that some folks will need long-term care, and that can be expensive. In a conversation with Kim Natovitz, president and founder of the Natovitz Group and a member of the individual solutions team at TriBridge Partners, I asked how decisions about long-term care insurance have affected her clients' retirement. With more than 25 years in the insurance industry, Kim has plenty of stories to tell.

She shared one example of a couple in their late 50s who had asked her about LTC insurance. Robert was self-employed while Ellen was a county employee; as an employee of the county in which they lived, Ellen was offered the opportunity to enroll herself and her husband in an LTC insurance plan. Kim evaluated the plan and encouraged the couple to apply for coverage, but they decided they were too young to need it yet. Unfortunately, within a year Ellen suffered an aneurysm and was hospitalized for many weeks in the intensive care unit. She eventually returned home but has both cognitive and physical deficits. Ellen's disability benefits will cover a portion of her lost income, but the couple will need to pay for her long-term care out of pocket.

Robert's business has been impacted significantly during his wife's prolonged health crisis, and his income is unlikely to recover entirely. In addition, he had been receiving health insurance through Ellen's employer; she will qualify for Medicare because of her disability, but he will need to purchase his own health insurance (at a cost of about $11,000 annually) until he, too, qualifies for Medicare.

Kim described another couple, Beverly and Mike, who decided to divorce once they became empty nesters. They went through the collaborative process with advisors who suggested that, with the loss of a built-in caregiver and smaller nest eggs due to the division of assets, each should obtain LTC insurance.

Mike said he never wanted to go into a nursing home, so he opted not to purchase insurance, despite Kim's explanations that all benefits could be used for home health care. Several years later, he suffered a mild stroke and required help with daily activities. Because he cannot cover the cost of care on his own and does not have long-term care insurance, his adult children have been collectively helping to pay for his care. The money they are spending on their father's care is preventing them from adequately funding their children's college accounts and their own retirement accounts, likely creating negative financial impacts for these families far into the future.

There are a lot of what-ifs in thinking about long-term care insurance, and when we talk with clients, we lay out a variety of scenarios and discuss what could happen in different circumstances. In the end, as with any type of insurance, the decision is about risk: How likely is it that you will need paid long-term care services? Do you have the financial wherewithal to afford what you will need without LTC insurance? Are you comfortable drawing down your estate to pay for this care, if need be?

Virg Cristobal, CFP®, Certified Financial Planner™ practitioner and licensed insurance broker, of Cristobal Associates/Sagemark Consulting, says that some of his clients elect to essentially self-insure, figuring that they either won't need long-term care or that the amount they'll pay is less than they would have spent on premiums over the years. The biggest reason clients avoid carrying LTC insurance, he says, is that there's a fear or perception that they won't receive a benefit; it's a use-it-or-lose-it proposition. These days, though, Virg is presenting some of his clients with another option, a newer hybrid approach that combines long-term care insurance with life insurance or an annuity. While such policies typically require large up-front premiums, they can be effective in protecting you should you require long-term care. These policies can be complex, so be sure to have an independent advisor explain the pros and cons of any policy you might purchase.

In some cases, long-term care insurance may not make sense for you financially. We have several clients who have significant assets and a family history of robust health right up until the end of their lives, and they have opted not to purchase an LTC policy.

One of my clients, Peter, asked me every year for about 20 years whether he should buy long-term care insurance, and I would joke with him that he and his wife would actually *save* a lot of money if he moved into a nursing home. He lived in high style, and his expenses would have only gone down if he could no longer go out, travel, and buy everything that caught his eye. For him, an LTC policy did not make financial sense. We helped Peter feel secure by reviewing his portfolio and showing him how his assets and pension income would support him and his wife quite well if either needed long-term care. Peter passed away a few years ago at the age of 85, and he never did need LTC insurance.

Putting Plans in Place

Thinking about illness and death is not something any of us wants to do, so we tend to put it off. But making your wishes clear before a crisis happens is often the kindest thing you can do for your loved ones, and it ensures that your medical and financial affairs proceed as you'd like. Advance directives guide both family and doctors to the types of medical interventions you want and clarify who you empower to act on your behalf if you are unable to make decisions for yourself.

Not having your estate documents in good order is a major fail if something should happen to you or your spouse. We have seen this occur too many times; a person dies or is incapacitated and the family has no estate documents or has documents that are outdated. It causes enormous stress and in some cases is extremely expensive for the surviving spouse and family. If you have not updated your estate documents in the last three to five years, I strongly urge you to talk to an experienced estate attorney and your financial advisor and get this done.

Advance directives consist of two types of documents:

- **Living will.** A living will, sometimes called an advance health-care directive, details your preferences for life-sustaining interventions such as tube feeding and hydration, cardiopulmonary resuscitation, mechanical ventilation, or surgery.
- **Power of attorney (POA).** This document designates a trusted person to act on your behalf (as your "agent") if you are unable to do so. Different types of powers of attorney exist, with differing grants of authority. You may choose one person as your power of attorney for health-care decisions and a different person to handle financial matters. Any power of attorney can be made "durable" with the inclusion of language that automatically extends the agent's authority in the event you are incapacitated or mentally incompetent at the time the POA expires.

Depending upon the jurisdiction and on how the document is drafted, the POA may be effective immediately, or it may go into effect at a future point after a triggering event – this is known as a springing power of attorney because the document springs into action once it is needed.

Advance directives must be in writing, and each state has its own forms and requirements for creating these legal documents. Some states combine a living will and a medical power of attorney into one advance directive. Be aware, too, that the terminology may vary from state to state, so the POA designated to handle health care may be called a medical or health-care power of attorney, durable power of attorney for health care, or health-care proxy.

When choosing a medical power of attorney, select a person who understands your wishes and is prepared to honor them. Ideally, the person will feel comfortable questioning medical professionals, be able to understand the realities of the situation, and feel capable of making decisions as you would want.

A financial power of attorney can conduct your financial affairs if you are unable to do so. You should, of course, choose a person whom you trust completely to handle your financial matters in your best interest should you become incapable of making decisions for yourself.

Your power of attorney and your health-care providers should have copies of any advance directives. Your POA should also have contact information for your health-care providers as well as your financial and legal advisors, and should know how to access your important accounts. Make sure to keep your power of attorney document up to date, and designate a new POA if yours should become unavailable for any reason. You can also change your living will (advance health-care directive) after it's been executed; if you do update your documents, be sure that new copies are distributed and old ones destroyed. Your attorney and your financial advisor will be able to help you navigate the specific forms your state requires and be sure that all legal conditions are met.

Steps to Take After a Diagnosis

While advance directives are important for everyone, they are even more critical if you are diagnosed with a serious condition that is progressive. If you or a loved one are diagnosed with a disease that is likely to become debilitating, begin working with your advisor to adapt your financial and estate plans.

Your individual diagnosis will inform much of your planning. Find out as much as you can about how your disease is likely to progress – your needs will depend upon the nature of your symptoms and abilities. Will you be able to continue to work (if you are not yet retired)? Is it likely you'll need to alter your home environment so you can function well (for example, will you need to retrofit the space to accommodate a wheelchair or other equipment)? Are you going to need a paid caregiver to assist you with tasks of daily living? Will you need full-time nursing care at some future point?

Once you have information, share it with your financial advisor, who can modify your portfolio to account for the expenses you are likely to incur. This brings us back to the retirement funnels and your portfolio allocation that we discussed in Chapter 1. If you anticipate that your expenses will increase, you will likely want to adjust your portfolio strategy.

If you don't have advance directives in place, have them drafted now; if your advance directives have already been executed, review and revise them as needed in light of your health challenge. Specific conditions may require you to rethink the parameters in your living will; some interventions that you would not have wanted to undergo in an end-of-life situation may be necessary and temporary given a chronic illness. Talk with those you've designated as your powers of attorney, and make sure that they are still able to act as your agent – the task is likely to be more demanding given your diagnosis with a chronic or debilitating disease.

Healthy Aging

While a health crisis can occur at any time and is more probable as we age, there is also a great deal we can do to maintain our health – and possibly even improve some areas – as we grow older. Aging is a normal process, simply part of the natural trajectory for living things. Despite countless advertisements for foods, products, or programs that promise to "reverse aging," nothing currently know to science can fulfill those promises. Instead, think about how to age in a healthy way as you journey through your retirement years.

At any age, you can cultivate practices that help you feel better and enhance your quality of life:

- **Eat well.** Fueling your body with the right nutrients and maintaining a healthy weight can help you stay active and reduce the time you spend visiting the doctor. A balanced diet is especially important if you have been diagnosed with a chronic medical condition.

- **Stay active.** One of the most critical ways to preserve physical and mental well-being, regular exercise can help stave off or provide relief from common chronic health conditions, including heart disease, back or joint pain, diabetes, depression, and arthritis, among others. A workout that incorporates training in flexibility, strength, balance, and endurance can counter many of the effects of aging on your body.[5] Try new things like yoga or other classes at the local gym to keep exercise fun and engaging.

- **Exercise your brain.** Decline in some areas of thinking (mild changes in memory and a slowing of the rate at which new information is processed) is a normal part of aging, but research has shown that a lifestyle that includes mental stimulation slows cognitive decline. Any activity that keeps your brain busy is good for it, so read books, write, learn a new language, take a class, do crossword puzzles, or embark on some other new intellectual adventure.

- **Practice good sleep hygiene.** Older adults need seven to nine hours of sleep per night, just as younger people do, though they often get less.[6] Lack of sleep can cause irritability, memory lapses, depression, and even medical conditions such as diabetes and cardiovascular disease.[7] Turn off the TV, computer, and bright lights at least one hour before bedtime, and do not read from backlit devices such as electronic tablets or certain e-readers.

- **Nurture your relationships.** Many older people live alone and may feel isolated after retirement, loss of a spouse, health challenges, or the death of friends and former colleagues. Keep close emotional ties with friends and family, even if you are no longer living in the same area. Social communication platforms have made this easier – ask for a tutorial from your child or grandchild if you need one. And find an exercise buddy, someone who will go for a walk with you or get you to the gym every day.

- **Break poor health habits.** If you are a smoker, quitting may be among the best things you can do to improve your health. Health risks associated with smoking include heart attack, emphysema, lung cancer, and various other cancers.

Pay attention, too, to alcohol intake, and seek help if you feel that drinking has become a problem. Over time, excessive drinking can lead to liver and brain damage and certain types of cancers, as well as exacerbate conditions such as diabetes, hypertension, memory loss, and stroke.[8] In addition, alcohol can make you more prone to falls and other accidents, including car accidents.

Live Long and Prosper

If you are lucky, you will spend decades in retirement living the life you've planned. And sometimes we make our own luck – or at least give it a firm push – so commit to doing what you can to stay healthy for as long as possible. Ideally, you want your good health to last as long as your life does. Whatever your future holds, make sure that you are prepared to meet it by putting the proper safeguards for your health needs in place.

Make Sure You Are Covered

- Assess your insurance needs, both health insurance and long-term care insurance, and be sure you are adequately covered.

- Make certain your advance directives are in place (living will and power of attorney).

- Develop good health habits and attend to routine screenings and health maintenance as appropriate for your age and individual health profile.

- Enjoy your life, and make the most of your time with family and friends.

CHAPTER 8

Life's Unpredictabilities

During the Great Recession of 2008 and 2009, a lot of companies were scrambling because revenue was falling and profits were getting crushed. Families were also scrambling as wage earners lost their jobs; asset values for stocks, bonds, and real estate were cut in half; and, for many families, their debt grew greater than their assets (this was especially true of their homes). This was a global recession, and it affected everyone.

In 2008, most financial professionals and investors were not expecting the Great Recession, which impacted nearly all people and all investment assets. As a firm, we started to become more cautious with our investment strategy in the fall of 2007, based on our analysis of the economic outlook, and had reduced most clients' higher-risk assets, primarily stocks, by 20 to 50% by the middle of 2008. This strategy worked very well for our clients, though clients still lost some money during the downturn, as did almost every investor.

As is typical during recessions, many companies had to cut expenses and lay off employees. My family experienced this first-hand. Both my brother and my brother-in-law were laid off by their companies. Both were in their mid-50s at the time. Both were surprised but not surprised. They knew their companies were laying people off, though they hoped that the axe wouldn't fall on them.

But as my brother Bill said, "When sales are down dramatically, how many salespeople do you need?" He was in sales for a large computer company, and he was darn good at it. When companies with dramatically falling profits make decisions about who to cut and who to keep, they often retain the 30- and 40-year-olds, who are less expensive and have more working life left in them.

Although many companies were generous to their employees during the layoff, offering extended pay and benefits, the job loss still came as a shock – and it meant those who were suddenly unemployed had to figure out what came next.

The Great Recession was a brutal reminder that the best-laid plans often go awry. Sometimes you are rolling along through life and everything is unfolding according to design. You have a thriving career and a healthy income, you are investing wisely and saving for retirement, and the world seems like a pretty friendly place. But circumstances can change quickly, and you may suddenly be faced with a path much rockier than the one you'd set out on. While you can't, by definition, be fully prepared for the unexpected, there are steps you can take to ensure you are well positioned to travel the entirety of your journey as smoothly as possible.

In this chapter, we'll talk about a number of events that can potentially impact your retirement if you have not prepared adequately. While there are different solutions depending upon the scenario, one of the best ways to *ensure* your financial future is to *insure* yourself properly. Lack of proper insurance can mean that a crisis leads to outsize damage to your nest egg. Investing in appropriate life, disability, and umbrella insurance policies can help ward off financial woes when an accident strikes.

When we sit down with clients to do a financial independence analysis, we are looking down the road 20, 30, 40, or 50 years. We think we have a good plan. But then it is helpful to ask, "Okay, what could go wrong? What should we do to prepare for emergencies or unexpected events?"

Didn't See It Coming: Layoff and Early Retirement

One often-unforeseen life event is being forced to take early retirement. Data from the Employee Benefits Research Institute shows that 47% of people who retired had done so before they'd expected to, prompted by a disability, a layoff, or the need to become a caregiver to a family member.[1] Early retirement can have devastating effects on retirement plans, especially for high earners, because the last years of working life are typically the highest paying.

If you are forced into an early retirement, spend some time reviewing your circumstances. The reasons for your status will dictate some of your choices, of course; suffering an accident or needing to care for a loved one will require different actions than if you've been forced out of your job. But whatever your situation, you will need to reevaluate your plans and make necessary adjustments.

First, review your pension and your investments. Depending upon the level of assets you have and on how close you are to the age at which you'd hoped to retire, you may be wise to postpone withdrawing from your individual retirement account (IRA), 401(k), or other retirement accounts so that you can conserve what you have for the future.

You'll also want to take a look at any benefits you may be entitled to, such as Social Security, Medicare or other health insurance, and disability or unemployment benefits, if those are applicable. If you are not at an age where you are eligible to claim Social Security or Medicare, you will need to investigate other options. Disability insurance, which we'll discuss below, is critical if injury or debilitating illness is the reason for your premature retirement. (See Chapter 7, "Health Matters," for more on health insurance.)

Your best course will depend on what the review of your portfolio and benefits reveals – you may need to cut back on spending or bring in some additional income to close the gap your lost paycheck created.

Of course, the simplest prescription for replacing income after a layoff is to find a new job, but during difficult economic times or in faltering industries that is easier said than done. Reevaluate your skills and career possibilities, and consider part-time or consulting work to help extend your nest egg.

Your financial advisor can look at your cash flow and help you estimate how long your money will last. He or she can also make recommendations for spending and portfolio adjustments that are tailored to your needs.

As I mentioned earlier, my brother-in-law, Frank, whose assets we manage, was one of those executives who found himself laid off unexpectedly during the 2008 downturn. A senior-level manager at a large chemical company, he was in his mid-50s when he got the news that his position was being eliminated. During major recessions, companies often prune from the top, cutting loose relatively well-paid people in upper management. These businesses need to retain front-line employees to keep the company going, and they need a certain number of managers to organize and oversee the work, but typically they decide that many employees, particularly those well into their careers, can be sacrificed to cut expenses. A person in his or her 50s or 60s, usually at the peak of earning power, may have a tough time finding other employment that offers a comparable salary, especially during shaky economic times.

Fortunately for Frank, he and my sister had saved carefully and been prudent in their financial decisions. After a thorough review of their financial plan and retirement analysis, we concluded that they were financially independent and would be fine if Frank wanted to retire permanently. Their income sources and investment portfolio would be able to sustain them if they lived at their current lifestyle. That realization took a great deal of pressure off them.

Frank wasn't quite ready to stop working completely, so he eventually set himself up doing some consulting. He makes enough to cover some of the family's expenses and his work schedule is flexible, which leaves plenty of time for his real passion – trying to lower his golf handicap. Because they had planned well, were diligent with saving every year, lived within their means, and invested wisely, Frank and Pam were able to take his job loss in stride. In retrospect, they look at the layoff as a blessing in disguise because, without it, Frank would not have slowed down and they would not have begun to enjoy life as they do now.

My brother is a salesman, so he did fine. A smaller company scooped him up, and a year and a half later his previous employer needed an experienced salesperson and lured him back. Most of those who lost jobs in the 2008 financial crisis have since been rehired if they needed to work, but layoffs happen even absent a recession. Some industries are contracting, and companies are experiencing upheaval; and in the process even employees who felt relatively secure may be ousted. The experience causes many to stop and think: "My kids are heading off to college soon; do I need to rethink the type of financial support I can give them? Do they need to consider attending a state school rather than a private college?"; "Do I need to rethink housing? Maybe we should move to reduce our mortgage and property taxes"; "How close to the bone do we need to cut our expenses? Should I cancel our vacation?"

Sit down and do long-term tax and cash flow modeling, performing a retirement analysis that looks at all the permutations given your specific situation. Look at your assets and expenses, both current and projected, to see what the picture looks like, assuming you don't get a replacement job. And look at a scenario in which you get a job that is much lower paying. What will you be able to spend? How long will your money last? Model the likely scenarios, so you can take a clear-eyed view of the situation and understand what your options are. And look at the picture not just for 2 or 3 years, but for 10, 15, or 20, so you can see how it all may work out over the long term.

Disability

Sometimes, people have an interruption – either a short one or a long-term or even permanent one – in their work lives because they have an accident or contract an illness that prevents them from carrying out their job's essential functions. People are far more likely to be injured during their work lives than to die before retirement age, yet most people are more concerned with carrying life insurance than disability insurance.[2]

After I graduated from Penn State, I moved to the Washington, DC, area and rented an apartment. My next-door neighbor, Jeff, and I quickly became friends. Jeff was a young doctor, and I was a CPA working for Ernst & Whinney, now Ernst & Young, one of the Big Four accounting firms. Jeff would ask me tax questions, and I started going to him for my annual physical. What better way to build a 40-year friendship?

So what does all of this have to do with disability? Many years later, Jeff developed a nerve problem in his right hand. He was consulting doctors about it and was concerned that he would not be able to continue his medical practice.

Fortunately, Jeff had a strong disability insurance policy. Unlike many disabilities, Jeff's didn't have a sudden onset. In his condition, the nerve damage progresses slowly over time. The stress created by the slow progression and the uncertainty over whether he would be able to practice and whether he would actually qualify for disability payments was significant. Jeff had the right type of policy – what is called an "own-occupation" policy – which covers him if he cannot perform his work in his specialty; he doesn't have to be incapable of performing any occupation or job. Because he had good insurance in place, he was able to enjoy a healthy retirement. Without this policy, it would have been very difficult, if not impossible, for Jeff to retire early and continue his current lifestyle.

Disability insurance is critical to maintaining your financial stability in the event that you cannot work, and you must have a policy with the right definitions in place to gain the maximum benefit. As we saw with Jeff, if you develop a disability or suffer a serious accident that limits the use of your hands or degrades your cognitive abilities, you may still be able to work, just not in the career for which you were educated. You may be perfectly capable of selling men's suits at a department store, for example, but that job will not compensate you for the loss of your income if you had been a neurosurgeon or a litigator. In most instances, you should choose an own-occupation policy because it will cover you in the event you are unable to perform the occupational tasks in the career you have trained for.

Additionally, make sure your tax accountant includes the insurance premiums as income each year on your tax return. This may cost you a few dollars in taxes, but by doing so you ensure that any disability income you receive each year will come to you tax free. What a huge relief that was for Jeff when he started collecting his disability checks.

While the company you work for may offer group disability insurance, it is wise to review the policy and make sure the definition of disability is appropriate given the work you do. If not, you might want to invest in your own insurance policy to make sure you are properly protected. A qualified agent can walk you through the many options available, but in most cases we recommend a policy that begins paying three or six months after your disability begins (this period is called the elimination period) and continues until you turn 65 or 66.

Coverage that is equal to 60% of your pretax income should be sufficient in most cases; this amount is typically roughly equal to your take-home pay. Your financial advisor or insurance agent will also be able to help you identify whether you should explore high-limit disability insurance. These policies are designed for highly compensated professionals such as actors, sports stars, and marquee musicians, as wells as high-level business executives, attorneys, and physicians.

While you hope you will never need to call on your disability insurance, you will be relieved to have it should you suffer a disabling injury or illness.

In the United States, a disabling accident occurs every second,[3] and one out of every four US employees will suffer a disabling injury before retirement.[4]

Do I Still Need Life Insurance?

Patrick had just turned 55 when he received news that his cancer was terminal. His doctors gave him a likely lifespan of six to nine months, and told him he should get his affairs in order. Patrick did not have a financial advisor but was very good about tracking the family finances, and he had a life insurance policy in place. Now he wondered whether he had enough life insurance to care for the family.

Patrick and his wife, Lucy, were struggling with their sense of the coming loss. Patrick had just been hitting his stride with his company and was heading into his best earning years. His cancer treatments were difficult, but he seemed to be responding. Maybe there would be a miracle?

Patrick made it past nine months, then one year, then the second year. He far exceeded his doctors' expectations, but after a two-year battle, his body finally gave out. Lucy came to us for help and guidance. She wanted to know: Are we going to be alright? Will our three children be able to stay in their private school? What about college costs? Are we going to be able to stay in our home?

While death is as predictable as, well, taxes, the precise date of our demise is, for most of us, an unknown. And being prepared to care for the family you leave behind in the event that you die prematurely is part of mitigating life's unpredictabilities. Even if you live well into old age, you may still wish to carry life insurance for estate planning purposes.

Whether or not you need to maintain a life insurance policy is a question that depends upon your individual circumstances. If no one else relies upon your income, such as a spouse or minor children, and you have liquid assets that will cover immediate debts and expenses, you may not need to carry life insurance. There are still a few good reasons to have life insurance, however, and we will talk about these a little later.

If you have children or a spouse who depends on your income, you will need to be sure that you have enough coverage to ensure that their needs are met if you should die. The payout from the life insurance policy replaces your income and helps your loved ones meet living expenses, pay for college, or meet other financial obligations. The amount of insurance you carry will depend upon your situation: An older person with fewer long-term obligations is likely to need less coverage.

Had we met Patrick and Lucy sooner, we would have suggested Patrick carry significantly more life insurance to support the family. Lucy and the kids were going to be fine, as they had a good base of assets along with the insurance proceeds, but she was confronted with some difficult financial decisions. She did not want to take the kids out of private school right away and disrupt their lives further at such a tough time. We suggested Lucy keep life as normal as possible for the next year or two, but then she would have to take the difficult step to sell the house and find a less expensive home, and she would need to go back to work. This was very stressful, but she handled it just fine and made the necessary changes. She moved closer to family, and the kids are doing quite well.

If you are married, with or without children, ask yourself how well your spouse would fare without your income. Even if you don't have children, you and your spouse may have a mortgage, credit card debt, and other financial obligations that your spouse would have difficulty meeting on one income.

If you have kids, the stakes are even higher. Would your spouse be able to maintain the kind of life you want for your children without the help of your income? Will your kids' dreams of college be foreclosed without financial help from your life insurance policy, should you pass away early? And if the stakes are high for most parents, they are stratospheric for single parents, who must provide chief or sole support for their children. Do you have adequate coverage to make sure that the guardians you've designated for your children will be able to care for them properly?

And while many kids who are older – in college or nearly through – will probably not be dependent much longer, those with special needs may require financial support from you well into their future.

While many couples in which one spouse stays out of the workforce to care for the home and/or the children decide that the stay-at-home spouse does not need life insurance, Jon Katz, principal and founder of Virginia Medical Plans/Katz Insurance Group, notes that this is not always the case. The spouse at home contributes valuable work to the household, and that work will have to be paid for if the spouse dies. Also, Jon points out that, in the case of prolonged illness of the stay-at-home partner, a working spouse may have taken significant time off to care for his or her partner. The death benefits of the stay-at-home partner can replenish the remaining spouse's retirement nest egg, which may have been significantly diminished during the period of illness.

Jon notes, too, that sometimes totally unexpected situations arise, making it unwise to have dropped all life insurance coverage at retirement. He recounts the story of a client who, upon reaching retirement age, believed he no longer needed life insurance. This client dropped all of his coverage, but unfortunately divorced at the age of 75. A court-ordered condition of the divorce was a life insurance policy to indemnify the settlement. Because of his age and health history, he scrambled to find coverage and ended up paying $25,000 per year in premiums. While this scenario is far from common, the story underlines the care with which you should evaluate your decisions regarding life insurance.

How much life insurance do you need in place to protect the future of your spouse or partner and any dependents? What type of insurance should you consider? What lifestyle changes are you prepared to make if your spouse or partner passes away unexpectedly? These are some of the key questions you and your financial advisor should be discussing.

While there are many different types of life insurance, they typically can be categorized as either permanent or term: Permanent insurance is lifelong protection that pays out upon the death of the policyholder, as long as the premiums have been kept up to date and there have been no loans or withdrawals against the policy; term insurance offers protection for a defined period of time and pays out only if the policyholder dies during the term of insurance.

Permanent insurance (such as whole life, variable life, universal life, and others), while more expensive than term insurance, builds cash value over time, and it accumulates on a tax-deferred basis. Sometimes it is best to carry a mix of insurance policies. Many permutations of each product type exist, and the right policy will be the one that best matches your goals.

There are many more sophisticated tools we use to assess the overall insurance plan, but a simple way to think about life insurance needs is with the following formula:

Income × 20 − Investment assets + Debt + College costs

= Amount of life insurance

That gives you a dollar amount to start with.

For example, let's say we have a couple who has an annual income of $250,000 and two kids not yet in college. College costs are calculated at $30,000 to $50,000 per year for four to six years; for our purposes, we'll assume four years at $50,000 per child, so $400,000. This couple has investment assets worth $1.5 million and debt (mortgage, cars payments, and other debts) of $1 million.

$5,000,000 ($250,000 × 20) (for income replacement)
 − $1,500,000 (investment assets) + $1,000,000 (debt)
 + $400,000 (college costs) = $4,900,000 (recommended insurance coverage)

Depending upon the individual circumstances, we often recommend, instead of purchasing whole life or variable life insurance with higher premiums, purchasing lower-cost term insurance and investing the difference in a well-diversified investment account. We may also recommend purchasing two or three different term insurance policies so that, as your insurance needs decline, you can eliminate one policy.

In addition to providing for the needs of the family you leave behind, life insurance can serve estate planning purposes. Particularly for high-net-worth individuals, life insurance can help pay the estate tax or assist with dividing assets among beneficiaries. If your estate is less than $11.2 million ($22.4 million for a married couple), there should be no federal estate tax. Estates larger than these will pay an estate tax rate of 40%. For these large estates, strategies such as setting up irrevocable life insurance trusts or grantor-retained annuity trusts can help preserve the value of your estate or pass additional assets on to your beneficiaries.

Virg Cristobal, CFP®, Certified Financial Planner™ practitioner and licensed insurance broker, of Cristobal Associates/Sagemark Consulting, notes that many of his clients rely on benefits from life insurance policies to equalize the value of their estates. For example, one of his clients, a widow, owned several properties, which she wanted to leave to her adult sons, both of whom were married with children. One property, however, was worth much more than the other, and the two would appreciate at different rates. After taking into account the appraisals and calculating the rate of appreciation for each property, Virg secured a life insurance policy for his client that would pay out in an amount that allowed the son named as beneficiary to inherit the same amount as his brother who was willed the more valuable real estate. This was a great solution that helped to equalize the inheritance for each child. Of course, this particular option may not be suitable for all situations – your advisor can guide you to the best solution for your particular circumstance.

Get Documents in Order

Making sure that adequate life insurance is in place is a prime goal in safeguarding the future of our loved ones. But there are other tasks that must be attended to as well.

Often, in financial (and other) matters, one spouse takes charge while the other takes a more passive role. For many couples this is simply a division of labor or aligns with the particular partners' strengths, but both parties must be aware of the broad strokes of their financial picture and be able to access necessary documents and accounts should one spouse pass away unexpectedly or be incapacitated by an accident or sudden illness.

We also want to make certain that all estate planning documents are in order and that the proper trustees and beneficiaries are named on each asset. We suggest getting the proper documentation from your company retirement plans and any other holdings, so we can review beneficiary designations carefully; we like to see it on paper, so there are no surprises down the road. This is particularly important if a client has had two or three marriages. More often than I'd care to say, we get the paperwork and then say to the client, "It looks like your ex is named as the beneficiary on your 401(k) plan." Typically, they think they've changed it – and they may have, but the change may not have gone through. In any case, it is wise to be completely sure the beneficiary designations are as you want them.

There are different ways to set up the designations, but most people will name the surviving spouse and then the children, or perhaps the spouse and a trust for the children. Widows or widowers without children may name other relatives such as siblings, nieces, nephews, or cousins. Those people who have large estates and are charitably inclined may, instead of designating family, choose to give certain assets such as IRA accounts to a charity because it can be more tax efficient.

Make Sure to Carry an Umbrella

When thinking through all the things that could happen in the course of life and how we might protect our clients from potential fallout, one of the simplest things to do is to review liability coverage. We recommend that our clients carry umbrella insurance, which is liability insurance that provides coverage above the limit of what homeowners or automobile insurance policies cover. Essentially, its purpose is to protect your assets from unpredictabilities that appear in the form of injuries or property damage for which you are held liable or to pay for legal defense if you are not found liable.

When I talked with Diane Beatty, managing director of private client services at CAL Insurance & Associates, about the importance of carrying appropriate levels of insurance, she shared several stories with me in which clients who could potentially have faced devastating financial consequences had been protected by well-constructed insurance policies.

In one scenario, the young adult son of a client had hosted friends at his parents' backyard pool, with a tragic end. Diane likes to say that pets, pools, and parties equal problems, and many losses stem from those elements. In this case, the son, Eric, had invited a few people over for a late-night swim, not realizing that one guest had mixed alcohol and illegal drugs earlier in the evening. She drowned in the pool after being left alone for a few minutes.

Because Eric's parents were asleep just a few yards away and the death occurred on their property, they were sued by the young woman's parents. Though the death was indeed heartbreaking, Eric had not been with the woman earlier in the evening and was unaware of what she'd ingested, a point the defense lawyer made as he argued that Eric and his parents should not be held responsible. The parents' umbrella policy covered not only legal defense costs but also the compensation ultimately provided to settle the matter. Without a quality umbrella policy in place, the family would likely have been on the hook for hundreds of thousands of dollars.

Depending upon the policy, umbrella insurance can also compensate you if you are injured by an at-fault uninsured or underinsured motorist and the driver's policy is insufficient to pay for your medical expenses. As I was talking with Diane, she reminded me of a client we shared, Leslie, who was an avid cyclist. Leslie had been seriously injured by a driver who hit several cyclists who'd been training together.

Diane pointed out that many people do not realize how low minimums for auto insurance are in some states. In California, where our client was struck, the driver's policy aligned with state minimums and paid only $15,000 for each person injured, with a limit of $30,000 for all. Fortunately for Leslie, she was well covered by her own insurance for an underinsured motorist event. She was able to turn to her auto insurance policy for half a million dollars and then to her umbrella policy for $5 million additional in excess underinsured motorist coverage.

Because of the extent of her injuries, which required more than a dozen surgeries to repair, she was unable to work, and may in fact never be able to return to a demanding career. The $5.5 million she carried in the event of such an accident means that Leslie does not have to worry about the financial implications of her high medical bills, and can focus instead on getting well. Such umbrella policies protect you if you are a pedestrian or cyclist injured by an uninsured or underinsured motorist, not only if you are involved in a motor vehicle collision, so even if you think you don't need it because you rarely drive, the policy may be well worth the investment.

According to the Insurance Research Council, 12.6% of motorists nationwide – close to 30 million drivers – are uninsured.[5]

But, of course, not all clients are as well prepared. Stafford Jacobs, assistant vice president at CAL Insurance & Associates, shared a story of one of his clients, an elderly woman who had resisted his advice to increase her auto insurance and to carry personal umbrella insurance. One day, as she was backing out of her driveway in her car, she hit and injured a neighbor. Because her insurance was insufficient to cover the judgment against her, she ended up having to sell assets and was forced to move into her daughter's home.

Fortunately, umbrella insurance is relatively inexpensive and can extend the liability limits of your other policies – homeowners and auto insurance but also insurance on a boat or a second home, if you have one. Be sure that your specific policy covers all your insurance needs, and review your insurance annually as well as when you add an asset such as watercraft or real estate.

We typically recommend that our clients purchase an umbrella policy that is equal to their net worth. Above a certain level, however, such insurance can be hard to get, and for high coverage amounts – above about $10 million – you may need a specialized insurance company that focuses on high-net-worth clients.

Protecting your wealth is essential to ensuring a healthy retirement, and personal liability insurance is a critical component. If you are not currently carrying umbrella insurance, contact your financial advisor and your insurance agent to discuss the type and amount of coverage you should invest in.

Rocky Economic Times

An economic downturn is another potential threat to financial security in retirement, but it, too, can be partially mitigated with the proper steps. Return on your investment will even out over time whether the negative years are in the first half of the time period or the last half, assuming you aren't making any withdrawals, as illustrated in Table 8.1.

The difficulty comes, however, if you are withdrawing from your portfolio during the years in which there are negative returns; that is, when downturns can be a problem. If you head into retirement during an economic slide and are pulling from a stock portfolio that is showing negative returns, you can bust that account. When you are

Table 8.1   Growth of $1.5 million.

Beginning balance	Scenario A $1,500,000		Scenario B $1,500,000	
	Annual return	Account balance	Annual return	Account balance
Year 1	22%	$1,830,000	-2%	$1,470,000
Year 2	7%	$1,958,100	-11%	$1,308,300
Year 3	12%	$2,193,072	-9%	$1,190,553
Year 4	-2%	$2,149,211	-4%	$1,142,931
Year 5	-11%	$1,912,797	7%	$1,222,936
Year 6	14%	$2,180,589	22%	$1,491,982
Year 7	9%	$2,376,842	12%	$1,671,020
Year 8	-9%	$2,162,926	18%	$1,971,803
Year 9	-4%	$2,076,409	9%	$2,149,266
Year 10	18%	$2,450,163	14%	$2,450,163
End balance	$2,450,163		$2,450,163	
End balance difference	$0			

taking distributions from an account that's all in stocks, you can truly disrupt your retirement.

Several analyses show the impact of withdrawing funds from an investment account and the rates of return. Table 8.1 illustrates the return on investment based on random investment returns on a $1.5 million portfolio. Scenarios A and B use the same annual returns, but the order of the returns is different in the two scenarios. Scenario A shows the investment balance when there are positive returns in the first several years, with negative returns in later years; Scenario B illustrates the investment balance when that portfolio has all of the negative returns in the first few years. As you can see, after 10 years the amount of money in each portfolio is exactly the same.

Table 8.2 looks at the same rates of return but shows a withdrawal of $60,000 per year; it's clear from this chart that when you take money out of the account and have negative returns up front, the value of your account will be impacted dramatically, even after 10 years, when the strong returns finally come along.

So we work to make sure, as clients get closer to the point where they will need to withdraw cash, that the portfolio is structured properly. This approach dovetails with the discussion in Chapter 1 on appropriate spending and how to prepare for financial independence in retirement. We recommend setting up the portfolio so

Table 8.2   Growth of $1.5 million with withdrawal of $60,000 per year.

| | Scenario A | | Scenario B | |
| | $1,500,000 | | $1,500,000 | |
Beginning balance	Annual return	Account balance	Annual return	Account balance
Year 1	22%	$1,770,000	-2%	$1,410,000
Year 2	7%	$1,833,900	-11%	$1,194,900
Year 3	12%	$1,993,968	-9%	$1,027,359
Year 4	-2%	$1,894,089	-4%	$926,265
Year 5	-11%	$1,625,739	7%	$931,103
Year 6	14%	$1,793,342	22%	$1,075,946
Year 7	9%	$1,894,743	12%	$1,145,059
Year 8	-9%	$1,664,216	18%	$1,291,170
Year 9	-4%	$1,537,648	9%	$1,347,375
Year 10	18%	$1,754,424	14%	$1,476,008
End balance	$1,754,424		$1,476,008	
End balance difference		-$278,418		

you have eight years of fixed income assets that you can draw from; that way, you won't be hit hard if you retire during a downturn. It's important to build in some time for the stocks to come back – you don't want to be selling on the downside. Depending on your assets, you may be able to live off the income from your portfolio, but that can sometimes be tough in a downturn. You always want a little buffer.

"Is there a disadvantage to this strategy?" clients will ask. The possible drawback is, of course, that you could have made more money by keeping a larger amount in equities if the market goes up rather than down. But you have to ask yourself whether the possibility of increasing your sizable nest egg is worth the risk of shrinking it dramatically. Assuming you are on track to retire with a comfortable level of assets, dropping by 50% carries far more negative implications than growing by 50% carries positive ones.

We follow economic indicators and market movements closely and plan according to the data we gather, but no one can know for certain the unpredictabilities the market will face; by shielding yourself from the worst effects of a downturn and giving your stock portfolio time to recover, you can offset some of the unknowns that may be lurking.

Another Unpredictability: Single-Stock Risk

In the 1990s we saw amazing wealth creation from companies that later fell hard or ceased to exist entirely when the tech bubble burst. I recall clients with significant investment in Cisco Systems who wanted more because this was going to be the company of the future. Unfortunately, to invest in the stock you had to pay an absurd 300 times earnings, when the long-term price would typically be around 16 to 18 times earnings. Cisco's price hit $82 per share in March 2000, up from 8 cents 10 years earlier (taking into account stock splits). I recall meeting with some prospective clients who decided not to hire us as their advisor because we would not purchase Cisco and a few other high-flying companies in their portfolio.

Cisco was the darling stock at the time, and – according to some of my prospective clients – you would have to be a fool not to own it. I would tell them I loved the company but didn't like the price. Nineteen months later, in October 2002, Cisco was at $8 per share, a whopping 90% loss.

I started working with Microsoft employees in 1988 and watched many of them hit the lottery with their stock options in the 1990s. Microsoft is a terrific company, but does that mean you keep all your eggs in its basket? A basket you don't control?

Fortunately, our clients followed our process for managing single-stock risk, and many of them are now happily enjoying an early retirement. Our process is simple: Look at the amount of risk you are willing and able to take, and then build a clear and consistent strategy for managing that risk.

During the bull market of the 1990s we would say, if you believe your stock will grow by 20 or 30% per year, then let's sell 20 or 30% of your stock and diversify into other assets, for risk management purposes. If the stock doesn't grow that fast, then you will be glad you diversified. And if the stock does grow as anticipated, you will still have the same amount of stock you started with. The strategy is not about saying which investment will do better; it is about creating some diversification in case the stock goes down dramatically – as Cisco did.

I watched as some potential clients thought we were being too conservative with our strategy. They went with a brokerage firm that had a strategy of borrowing against the stock and stock options. Their thinking was, why sell a stock growing at more than 30% per year when you can borrow against the stock at a 6 or 7% interest rate? On paper, the analysis was brilliant, but it assumed you can control all the outcomes. We wouldn't take the bait and lost those prospective clients when we told them that it was not a risk worth taking.

Unfortunately, in 2000 when the tech bubble burst, many of those multimillionaires went broke. They sued the brokerage firm they'd gone with for talking them into making those trades. And they lost again. Don't let greed get in the way of a great retirement. Make sure you have a clear process in place for making decisions that will help you reach your long-term goals.

Often, people are reluctant to sell company stock in which they have significant investment because they (or their family) have built the company and they are emotionally attached to their investment; they may be privy to the details of fundamentals and have faith that the company is solid, or they may feel that the historic strong performance of the stock is an indicator that it will continue to soar. But there are no guarantees, and those who are unwilling to diversify may face unhappy consequences down the road. A concentrated position in a single stock presents a substantial risk. The stock may have been the source of your good fortune, but it can just as easily lead to financial disaster.

Even large companies that appear to be stable may suffer sudden losses due to idiosyncratic risk – specific risks associated with the particular circumstances of a company or industry. It happens more often than you may think. When a company is hot, it may be the darling of Wall Street, but two years later it is struggling or even out of business altogether – remember Pets.com, Sharper Image, Lehman Brothers?

If you keep all your eggs in one basket, you risk being devastated if that basket gets smashed. I had a client, heavily invested in company stock, who wanted to build a multimillion-dollar home. I told the couple they didn't want to sign on a high-priced real estate deal while sitting on that stock – it's too risky if the stock price drops – but the husband didn't want to sell because the stock was doing so well. "Why get off the winning horse right now? Let's keep riding while the horse is winning," he told me. I asked him whether jeopardizing their retirement, which was right around the corner, was worth gambling that the stock would keep rising.

I told the clients firmly that if I were in their position, I would sell the stock and begin construction on my dream home; but if they were not ready to sell the stock, they should not sign a commitment to buy the land and build the house. Husband and wife deliberated for a couple of days, and then the wife called me and said, "We are going with your advice. We hate to sell the stock right now, but we have to trust that you know what you are doing. And we want the house and we want to retire soon."

As luck would have it, we sold near the all-time high stock price, at about $90 per share. Just two years later it was $15 per share. Not only did our clients get their dream home, they are happily enjoying their retirement. But neither of these things could have happened had they not made the decision to sell the stock.

Clients who have a lot of their assets tied up in a single stock often joined the company as it was taking off, and they did very well; these are Facebook, Twitter, and Google folks. But gaining a windfall through company stock is like winning the lottery. I ask these clients, "If you won $10 million in the lottery, would you invest all $10 million in more lottery tickets?" Of course they wouldn't. But every day you don't sell the stock is a day you've chosen to hold it, which means, essentially, that you've bought it. You may feel emotionally invested in the success of the company and unwilling to believe it's ever going to turn, but threats to the company can and do pop up unexpectedly.

The most obvious answer is to sell some shares and diversify into other assets, and that is a strategy we pursue when possible. Sometimes, though, the matter is not so simple. Clients may have reasons that they need or want to hold onto the securities; possibly, the stock cannot be sold until a certain date or event, or the client may want to maintain a certain percentage so as to preserve voting rights or other interests. If that's your situation, your financial advisor can look at your particular circumstances and choose alternative option strategies that will help you to minimize single-stock risk, even if you must continue to maintain a significant position.

Family Needs

For most people, taking care of family comes above any other desire or commitment they have. When we meet with clients, we always talk about the possibility that they will need to provide ongoing support to some family members. Will they, for example, need to offer financial or physical support to their aging parents or provide for children who may not be fully self-supporting?

It's typically easier to forecast the needs of clients' parents because they are most likely in or near retirement. If the parents are willing to share information about their financial health, we can estimate the likelihood that clients will need to set aside money to contribute to their care down the line.

With regard to children, the calculation is often more difficult; a hardship or a disability can be a surprise when it happens. My brother called me to see if I could help a close friend whose daughter has a debilitating disease, a diagnosis she did not receive until she was in her twenties. While they are in excellent financial shape and helping with their daughter's care will not jeopardize their retirement from a financial perspective, her care could cost a significant amount of money.

Fortunately, though the daughter had to quit her job and move near her parents, she has been able to keep health insurance because of the 2010 Patient Protection and Affordable Care Act (known as the ACA or Obamacare). The future is uncertain, however, and depending upon the disease's progression, their plans for life in retirement may need to change, and they may choose to alter their financial and estate plans to accommodate ongoing care for their daughter once they are gone.

Sometimes that unexpected thing happens when the child is younger, or even before birth. Children with autism or serious developmental delays, as well as those with physical disabilities or mental illness, may benefit from specialized educational opportunities and care; while many public resources are available, there are also some that are costly or scarce. Experimental therapies are often not covered by insurance, and families may wish to pay out of pocket for such treatments, perhaps adding to the financial strain.

When a child has significant needs, much of life can be consumed in making sure that those needs are met, and it can be difficult for a family to function normally. In addition to financial stress, there can be strain in the relationship and guilt associated with depriving other children of attention.

Quite often, people whose kids have special needs are younger; they're in their 30s or perhaps even younger. In this case, their lives are altered forever; earning capacity may be much lower, as one parent stays at home to care for the child. If parents hire a caregiver, a qualified person may be very expensive. The situation can be challenging for retirement planning, and emotionally draining for people around the family.

This is where grandparents may come in. If grandparents have some wealth, they are usually inclined to help as they can, financially and sometimes by stepping in and providing some care.

As we discussed briefly in Chapter 2, for a child who is going to require continuing support, parents or grandparents may set up a special needs trust for the child's future care. This requires careful attention because these trusts must take into account the particular financial circumstances and likely future needs of the beneficiary; supplemental care special needs trusts are designed so as not to jeopardize state or federal support the child or grandchild may be entitled to, such as Social Security, Medicare, or Medicaid. If the trust is written correctly, the child will be able to receive those benefits. An estate attorney with experience in special needs trusts should put together the documents, and your financial advisor can review to be certain that the financial and tax implications have been fully considered.

The special needs trust can function as a savings tool for your child's future. You may not have a big pot of money right now, and your child may be young, but you can make deposits into a special needs trust just like you save in a 401(k) or IRA. The trust may also be funded by money or property left in a will.

With a little planning as events unfold, you can prepare for the health needs and future well-being of family in a way that protects their interests and maximizes your contributions.

Predicting the Future

There are many events we call accidents that are not entirely unpredictable. According to the Bureau of Transportation Statistics, there were an estimated 5.6 million highway accidents in 2012 (the most recent year these figures were available); statistically, a driver is likely to be involved in three or four vehicle collisions over a lifetime.[6] Car crashes happen with regularity, yet you never intend them and on any given day you are not likely to think you will be in a collision. In the same way, you do not plan for your deck to collapse during a party or for your spouse to die before you, but these things happen to people every day.

The best thing you can do to offset the negative effects of calamity is to assess your vulnerabilities and protect yourself with good insurance and strong contingency plans. Because you can't predict when you might need insurance, or for what exactly, carrying appropriate levels of disability, life, homeowners and auto, and umbrella liability coverage reduces your chance of outsize financial loss if the unexpected should happen. Likewise, you cannot predict what stock returns will be or if your company will hit a major pothole and spin out of control. When making financial decisions, you should have a process and a plan that takes these variables into consideration.

Expecting the Unexpected

- Disability insurance can reduce your risk of financial trouble if you become disabled and cannot work for a prolonged period of time. Policies can be customized so that they cover your particular career ("own occupation") and extend until you reach retirement age.

- Consider whether life insurance can further an estate planning goal or protect your family from the burden of your unpaid debt. It can also replenish lost income for a caregiver spouse, in the event an insured spouse dies after a lengthy illness.

- Review your insurance policies annually to be sure that you are well covered. A qualified agent, along with your financial advisor, will be able to conduct the review efficiently and let you know whether you are in good shape.

- Plan for the needs of family members who may require extra support. If you have a child with a disability, a special needs trust can provide for his or her future care. Be sure to consult estate planners and financial advisors who have experience in this specialized area.

- Evaluate your investment portfolio and see what market risk you are taking. If you are withdrawing from your portfolio or have a significant position in a single stock, make sure you have a plan that protects against major market moves to the downside.

CHAPTER 9

Underliving Your Wealth

One Sunday, years ago now, I was visiting my parents for dinner. My mom and dad loved to travel, and they had recently returned from a four-week luxury tour of Europe. As they were telling me about their trip through the great capitals of the continent, my mom set a salad bowl on the table and explained that there were no tomatoes in the salad because tomatoes were too expensive at the store.

I love to share that story because it illustrates perfectly people's idiosyncrasies about money. My parents had just taken a very expensive vacation, which they enjoyed tremendously, but a high-priced tomato was just too extravagant. It's not that they couldn't afford it; they just weren't willing to spend on something they thought wasn't worth the price. We all place different value on things, and we are constantly making judgments about what we consider a fair exchange for various items and experiences. A lifelong city dweller might not have given a second thought to buying tomatoes at the price my mother refused. But Mom had grown up on a farm, and to her, $4 per pound for tomatoes (or whatever the price was that day) was just too much.

I find myself doing the same thing. I often skip lunch because I'm running too hard during the day, so my wife, Pam, has recently begun making lunch for me to take to work. At the end of the day I come home with the paper bag and she asks what I'm doing bringing home a used paper bag. I say, "It's perfectly fine, I can use it again tomorrow." I'll spend freely on a nice dinner out, but a deeply ingrained sense that I should reuse what I can means that I take the trouble to fold up my paper lunch bag and stick it in my briefcase for a second use. In the scheme of things, will the few pennies I save on lunch bags

136

make any appreciable difference to my savings? Nope. But that type of small economy is a quirk I have, left over from my upbringing. I tell Pam, "That's the Pittsburgh in me." We grew up with hand-me-downs and threw nothing away if it still had a thread of future use. That was a family value, and it's one I still have.

Every single person I've ever met has a few eccentricities in the way he or she handles money. And that's okay. In fact, it's healthy to stop and think about your purchases, and to consider whether what you're buying is (a) truly something you want or need and (b) worth what you're spending on it. But it's also important to balance your quirky frugalities with a realistic sense of what you can spend and to enjoy what you've worked so hard for.

Amazingly, underliving their wealth is a big reason many people fail at retirement. We've focused up to this point on the traps that can jeopardize your financial independence, but you can also stunt your retirement by being afraid to appreciate the fruits of your labor. After all, retirement is not just the end of one phase of your life – a phase in which you built a career, likely raised a family, and contributed to your community. It's the beginning of a new phase – one in which you can explore areas you were too busy to investigate before. But, for a variety of reasons, people sometimes fail to live fully in their retirement years and enjoy what they have built.

Your Money Personality

The way you think about and handle your money is based on a complicated mix of your personality and your upbringing – on the way your parents and other family thought about money and whether there was a lot or a little in your household, as well as the economic context of the time and place where you grew up.

While there are many variations and ways to categorize different money personalities, the personality types generally fall into three main categories: Spenders, avoiders, and savers. Spenders get pleasure from buying items and services for themselves and others, and they may have a difficult time holding onto cash; avoiders dislike thinking about money, either because they feel overwhelmed and intimidated or because they have a sense that money can be corrupting ("the root of all evil"); savers feel more secure when they have a sizable amount of money at their disposal, and some may tend toward hoarding their wealth. There is, of course, a wide range of behaviors within each category, and those at the extremes may have disordered thinking about their finances.

We talked about spending in Chapter 1, focusing chiefly on problem spending. But saving or conserving at the extreme can be an issue, too, particularly if you are financially comfortable but consider spending on vacations, entertainment, and even the occasional luxury to be risky or ill-advised.

According to a 2015 survey, 15% of affluent investors regret not enjoying their money more.[1]

Living with Fear

Fear is probably the biggest reason people underlive their wealth. They think, "Something bad could happen, so I have to constantly protect what I have." They fear that they could run out of money – that the markets could take a dive, the value of their property could tank, or they'll run through their savings too quickly.

This anxiety runs through even some very wealthy clients, whose portfolios are robust enough that they could sustain themselves through nearly any downturn. These folks could easily afford to travel or to indulge their interests in whatever ways they choose. But old habits die hard, and irrational fear of the future may take hold; sometimes people in retirement remain in full-on save and conserve mode even when there is no rational reason to do so.

In physical terms, the inclination to hoard money is not unlike the mentality of doomsday preppers who store up seven years' worth of food and water in the event that society breaks down. While it's wise to be prepared for emergencies, don't let yourself be so busy worrying about things that will probably never happen that you forget to live.

When we encounter clients who think they are at great risk and so cling unnecessarily to their cash, we try to help them manage their fear. To help dispel the worry we look at the overall picture, both at history – at the performance of the markets over time – and at the clients' individual portfolio levels and allocations, to assure them that they are invested in a way that properly manages their risk.

While no one can guarantee smooth times ahead, we can make projections and weigh the likelihood of various scenarios coming to pass, which tends to calm jitters enough that people can go ahead and live as they wish. If cautious spending is their true preference, that is fine, but if our clients aren't enjoying themselves because they are afraid they can't afford it, a candid picture of their finances can often set them at ease and help them take pleasure in what they've worked so hard to earn.

When Money Personalities Collide

It's common for couples to argue over money and how to spend it. If one person falls into one category of money personality and the other falls into a different category – or even if the two are in the same category but at opposite ends of the spectrum – conflicts may arise. The way you handle money is, after all, very personal, and it's easy to feel attacked when your partner questions your decisions to save or spend.

Quite often, fear regarding spending manifests mainly in one spouse or partner. It's not unusual for one partner in the couple to really believe that they are in danger of outliving their wealth and to live off that fear. That partner has a habitual pattern of thinking about money that goes like this: "Everything that can go wrong *will* go wrong, so we'd better not spend any money we don't have to."

A 2015 Fidelity study found that more than one-third of couples disagree on the amount of their household's total investible assets (36%).[2]

I have a client couple who fits this profile. The husband is fearful that another recession or even a depression is coming and that they will be all but wiped out, but the wife wants to get out and explore the world now that they have the time. They worked really hard at their careers their whole lives, they are very well situated financially, and it's really only the husband's apprehension that is holding them back.

When I spoke with this couple at a recent meeting, I told them, "You are spending $10,000 a month and can probably spend twice that amount without risking your future at all. What would you like to do?" I listed a few ways they might enjoy their money, and the wife's eyes sparked when I mentioned a trip to Australia. But her husband was hesitant, feeling that was an expensive trip that they didn't need to take right then.

In some instances, the fear is about leaving the other spouse alone and without adequate financial resources. My dad passed away early, leaving behind my mom, who was four years younger. His concern had always been that she would give everything away to the kids and then be broke. I manage her money for her, and she would occasionally remind me: "Dad always worried that I wouldn't have enough. Do I have to be careful?" My dad's warnings have stayed with her through the years. She grew up on a farm during the Depression years and remembers how lean times can get.

Here's the thing. At some point, it will likely be too late to truly enjoy many of the things you can do with your money. As you grow older, you may find it more difficult to travel comfortably. Even if you are relatively healthy and can physically make the trip, changes to your mind and body as you age may mean that you feel less enthusiastic about it. Possibly, you will be less able to get to the sites you want to see or to spend hours walking the streets of foreign cities. It will get more difficult to try new adventures. Do the things you want to do while you are young and healthy enough to enjoy them.

Planning for your financial future is critical, but if you and your advisor have reviewed your portfolio and you are within the limits of appropriate spending, get out and enjoy your wealth. Shortly after my meeting with the reluctant couple I just mentioned, I spoke with the husband, who told me they'd booked a three-week trip to Australia and New Zealand and he felt good about it.

Gifting

Ensuring that money is left as an inheritance for their children is a concern for some people, and we have clients who cite this as the reason they hold tight to the purse strings. While leaving a financial legacy is an important consideration, it's helpful to balance this desire with the need to enjoy family time while you are around to take pleasure in it.

We have a few frugal clients who are not particularly interested in travel or in buying art or real estate or other things that might bring them pleasure. Instead, their joy comes from family. When this is the case, we will ask, "Okay, when it comes to family, what's important to you?" We like to show them what their abilities are, suggesting possibilities like a family gathering that would help them make lasting memories with their children and grandchildren.

My parents went down this path, and one year they rented a couple of beach houses for a few weeks. They invited all of their kids and grandchildren to join them, and they covered the expenses. That was hard for any of us to turn down, especially early in our careers when we didn't have a lot. The vacation was a huge success. Extended family came down to stay when they could, and my parents took great satisfaction in seeing the whole clan having a good time together. They repeated this most years, always coming up with a new place and a new adventure.

These sorts of experiential gifts are a good way to spend in accordance with your values and share your time and wealth with those you love. People are sometimes afraid to do this until we start walking them through it, but then they get excited by the prospect.

We do have a few clients who have wondered whether they should just conserve everything and will their children the entirety instead of spending in this way. I say, "You are spending their inheritance on having special times with them. You're not going to get through it all." A common worry is: But maybe they don't want to spend it that way. To which I reply, "What do *you* want?"

I've seen some situations where the kids have inherited a great deal of money, and they don't even feel good about it because their parents didn't enjoy it. The kids felt guilty. You do your children a favor by showing them how to enjoy life and not make an obsession out of saving every dollar.

Once my dad had passed away and my mom had reached her 80s, she began looking for a new way to show her love to her children and grandchildren. She is pretty conservative in her spending and has room in her budget to spend much more than she does. Her needs at this point are fairly simple, and she has a nice income and a portfolio that easily meets her cash needs. So what should she do with her money, especially now that her travel is limited?

After some discussion, we came up with the idea of "I love you" gifts for her grandchildren and great-grandchildren. Every now and then, she sends each a note with a check inside. She'll say to me, "How are my investments doing? I want to send my grandchildren some money to help them out."

The "I love you" gifts come out of the blue, which makes them a special surprise. I suggest keeping the gifts completely random – vary the amount, and don't tie them to a major holiday or to birthdays. The grandchildren are in their 20s and 30s now, and the gift means a lot to them. It takes a small financial burden off of them and lets them dream a little. And for my mom, it's a fun way to feel uplifted and give her grandchildren an unexpected treat.

So Enjoy . . .

Retirement is an opportunity to try new things, unencumbered by the demands of work and daily care for children. If you have enough wealth to be comfortable financially and to explore new places and activities, go and do it. As long as your spending is not jeopardizing your lifestyle and risking your becoming an eventual burden to your children, you should enjoy what you've worked so hard to achieve.

If you're not sure that your spending levels are appropriate to your retirement savings, consult a financial advisor who can analyze your portfolio and your needs and offer some recommendations. There is a possibility that you don't need to be quite as conservative as you think and that you can afford to take that trip or arrange an extended-family getaway.

Staying engaged in life is a critical part of a happy retirement, and it's important to remember that your money is a tool rather than an end in itself. So don't fail at retirement by underliving your wealth – this new chapter of your life gives you a chance to make the most of what you have and to share your good fortune with those you love.

Tips for Living Fully in Retirement

- Live within your means, but understand what that entails. If you have worked hard so that you can enjoy retirement and have a nest egg that will provide well for you, go ahead and explore the activities you would enjoy. Don't let fear limit your possibilities.

- Talk with your financial advisor about what you can safely withdraw for your spending and about a gifting strategy, if that is something you would like to do. Having a clear financial plan can bring peace of mind if you are anxious about outliving your money.

- Discuss your goals, both lifestyle and financial, with your spouse or partner, if you have one, to help resolve any differences in your money personality.

- Consider spending on experiences, especially those you can share with family. Research shows that people derive more happiness from spending on trips, entertainment, and special dinners out than on material items like TVs or cars.[3]

- Likewise, studies show that spending on others contributes to our own happiness, so go ahead and give those gifts. Just be sure not to create an expectation of a gift, and vary the amounts you give each time (remember, this is a gift, not an entitlement). What better way to enjoy your wealth than by surprising family with "I love you" gifts?

Finding the Right Financial Advisor

Before you begin your search, ask yourself: Why am I looking for a financial advisor? Perhaps an event, like a big promotion, the sale of your company, or an inheritance, means that you are now working with a significant amount of money and you want some investment and tax advice. Or, after reading this book, you may realize that you need a clear plan so you can avoid your own retirement fail. The reasons are always personal and are often specific to your situation.

Knowing your motivation, you can now start the search process. What makes a client-advisor relationship successful? What are the key criteria you should consider? What do you do to make the relationship special? Following are seven key characteristics of a great advisor-client relationship. (At the end of this section you will find a checklist you can use as you start your search.)

You Trust the Advisor

Trust is table stakes, or the necessary basis of your relationship. Your wealth advisor is going to be one of the key people who will have knowledge of, and even some control over, your family's financial well-being. When meeting with a potential advisor, listen to your head and your gut. What is the overall feeling you get? Do you feel that this advisor has a passion for excellence as well as a high level of integrity and professionalism?

Of course, it is difficult to assess trust in a single meeting, but listen for the motives of the advisor. The advisor should be interested in understanding your goals and pulling out the specifics and complexities of your situation. Be especially wary of quick jumps to solutions. If the advisor receives commission, she may be motivated to steer you toward products or services that serve her interests rather than yours. Look for advisors whose priority is offering excellent advice rather than making sales.

You need to trust the individual advisor, but perhaps more importantly, you need to trust the team you will be working with and the overall institution. In today's scandal-ridden climate, a mismanaged firm can put your accounts and security at risk. Consider the overall reputation of the firm, awards or recognition from the investment community, and number of years providing objective, independent advice. Rankings from sources such as *Barron's, Forbes,* and *Washingtonion* can be a useful place to start, but be wary of financial advisors who tout the list as a valid source for how good they must be. SBSB appears on those lists, and I still say the rankings are helpful but should not be the final word in making your decision. Consider the awards and accolades the company has accumulated, but more importantly, look at the company you will be working with; can you put your full faith and trust in them?

The Advisor Listens and Cares

As we saw throughout this book, the real pitfalls of poor financial planning are often caused by matters of the heart. As time goes on, you will need to speak with your advisor about topics that you may not even confide to close friends or certain family members: Elder care for an aging parent, asset division in a divorce, the sale of a company, expenses for the care of a child with an addiction, and so on. You want to have these tough conversations with someone who can help and who listens and cares about you and your family. The world of personal finance encompasses much more than numbers and analysis.

In your face-to-face meeting with your potential advisor, do you feel like you are listening to a sales pitch, or is the advisor asking about what is most important to you?

Does the advisor address both you and your spouse? Often there is a "lead" person in the couple who feels responsible for the family investments and financial health. A good advisor will not focus on that person exclusively but will work to draw out all family members to ensure they understand, and that their needs and opinions are heard.

Who will you really be working with? Will you work with the person you are meeting with or will you be passed along to a different person? Will you have a single individual advisor or will you be working with a team? Unless your situation is relatively simple, you will most likely be better served by a team that has expertise in multiple fields such as investments and taxes, as well as in retirement, estate, and insurance planning. Ask about the team structure and the typical advisor-client communications.

The Advisor's Expertise Is Deep and Wide

By deep expertise, I am referring to the knowledge and years of real-world experience of your advisor. There are many designations in the financial services industry. The string of letters following an advisor's name can be confusing, and it can be tough to know the level of knowledge they truly signify. The top three designations you are likely to see are that of Certified Financial Planner™ (CFP®), certified public accountant (CPA), and Chartered Financial Analyst (CFA). You are probably most familiar with the CPA designation; professionals with this credential have expertise in the tax and accounting field. The CFP® designation shows a significant level of commitment and expertise in the broad area of financial planning, which can include planning for retirement, insurance needs, and estate planning, as discussed in this book. The CFA focuses on investment and security analysis and is helpful when creating your investment strategy. We strongly recommend that you choose advisors who have one or more of these designations.

When I say your advisor's expertise should be wide, I am referring to the larger team directly available to address your questions. For example, does your advisory team have a CPA available to address your tax issues? Is a CFA available to discuss more complex investment strategies and provide deeper analysis? Are the people providing your holistic financial planning properly certified as financial planners?

The Advisor Has Experience with Your Profession or Life Situation

As we saw earlier in the book, many professions or family situations can result in thorny financial issues. Even if your situation is relatively simple now, look ahead to the complexity you may have in the future. A 70-year-old retiree will have issues that are different from those of a young attorney, a budding entrepreneur, or a busy CEO. You want your advisor to have experience handling the specific issues that you face; you seek expertise in particular challenges when you see your doctor, attorney, or CPA, and you should expect the same of your financial advisor. For example:

- Attorneys need to pay special attention to quarterly tax payments, as well as tax issues that result from practicing in different states and internationally.
- Business owners may need help understanding the best pension plans for themselves and the insurance needed to shield them from business risks. Eventually, they may need advice for the big event of buying, expanding, or selling a business.
- Executives at large corporations need to manage the timing and amounts of company stock transactions. They are also extremely busy and need a resource that will handle their personal finances and be efficient with their time.
- Women tend to have a different view of wealth than men. They may need an advisor who will empower them with information and help them achieve goals that are meaningful to them.

Does the advisor you will be working with have clients with issues like yours? Can you speak directly to another reference client or two?

The Advisor Plays Well with Others

You want to have a financial advisor who is going to work well with the other professionals in your life, such as your estate attorney or tax accountant. Some firms do not have appropriate communication processes in place and struggle with sharing data and other critical information with complementary advisors. Seamless communication is especially meaningful when you want to get things done quickly or are confronting a challenging situation that requires thoughtful communication among all of your professional advisors.

The Advisor's Fees Are Clear and Transparent

You should be able to get a straight answer on the fees charged, the services included, and services that are not included from any firm you are considering working with. Before engaging any advisory firm, ask for a summary of fees and included services. If you are being charged a wealth-management fee that is a percentage of assets managed, is the financial planning included? How frequently is your financial plan updated? How are other services charged (tax preparation, if provided; estate planning and administration, if provided; and so on)? This is a good time to confirm who will provide the various services.

The Advisor Is a Forward-Looking Leader

There are many trends and new technologies in wealth management. Having a firm that looks forward as a leader and explores new opportunities to better serve its clients is important. Ask how the firm you are considering looks at future trends. Do the advisors understand new investment vehicles, and can they clearly explain why they do or do not invest in them? Are they utilizing state-of-the-art technology to protect your assets and information? Given constantly breaking news events, can they calm your fears by keeping you abreast of the impact on your investments and long-term retirement plans? Are they able to keep you updated on new laws and government policies, such changes to income and estate tax laws that may impact your retirement plans?

Your relationship with your financial advisor is among the most important ones you may ever have, so take the time to find the right advisor for you. You deserve an advisor you trust implicitly and who listens and cares about you, has the right experience to serve your needs, can work well with your other professional advisors, and is transparent about services provided and fee structures. An advisor with these essential qualities will be a great asset in looking out for your future and for the well-being of your family.

Checklist:
Finding the Right Advisor

Questions regarding the advisor:

- What designations? CFP®?
- Years of experience in wealth management
- Years with this firm
- Number of clients in your profession or life situation
- Will the advisor be your sole contact, or do you have a team to field questions?

Questions regarding the firm:

- How are advisors compensated?
- What is the average tenure of the advisors?
- Does the firm sell investment products/services?
- How long has the firm been in business?
- How are they regarded by the overall investment and financial planning community?
- How are the leaders compensated, and what is their growth model?
- What is the firm's investment philosophy? Can you speak directly to the investment team?
- Do they have tax expertise inside the firm? How do they account for tax consequences in investment trades and the like?
- How does the firm handle data security?
  - What does the company do to secure your financial data?
  - Is there a dedicated person on staff who is constantly looking ahead to risks and ways to secure your information and accounts?
  - Does the firm help inform clients of ways to protect data at home? How do they ensure that the rest of your family is protected?

- Does the firm have clients with professions or issues like yours? Can you speak directly to another reference client?
- How does the firm look at future trends?
- What are the fees? Are they transparent?

Questions to ask of a reference client:

- What is the response time to questions?
- Do you have access to the investment team?
- Do you feel the firm puts your interests first?
- Are they willing to work with other advisors (account, estate attorney, etc.) as part of your team, or do they see those advisors as competitors?
- Do they listen well? Do they include all members of your family in important decisions?

Questions specific to law firm partners:

- Does the firm have experience with other attorneys, and perhaps even with the specific plans at your firm?
- Can the firm help with planning and advice regarding cash flow issues?
- How do they deal with conflict-of-interest issues with attorney clients?
- Do they advise on tax issues?

Questions specific to entrepreneurs/business owners:

- Does the firm have experience with other business owners?
- Can they help with setting up owner pension plans or other savings vehicles?
- How much will they do to free up your time?
- Do they have experience in clients who are buying or selling a business?

Questions specific to corporate executives:

- Does the firm have experience with other corporate executives and perhaps even with your company?
- How do they address issues with being overinvested in company stock?
- How do they protect against liabilities and conflicts of interest?

About the Author

Greg Sullivan is the president and CEO of Sullivan, Bruyette, Speros & Blayney, and is a Certified Financial Planner™ professional and a certified public accountant (CPA) with more than 35 years of business, investment management, and financial planning experience. *Barron's,* a national financial publication, has recognized Greg as one of the nation's Top 100 Independent Financial Advisors and *Washingtonian* magazine named him as one of the Top Wealth Advisors in Washington, DC.

After earning his degree in accounting from the Pennsylvania State University, Greg started his career with Ernst & Whinney (now Ernst & Young). In 1991 he cofounded SBSB, a wealth management firm providing financial planning and investment advice to high-net-worth and ultra-high-net-worth clients. He and his partners later sold to Harris Bank, a subsidiary of Bank of Montreal, and partnering with these banks allowed Sullivan and his cofounders to expand their business. In early 2016, the SBSB partners repurchased the company from Bank of Montreal. The firm currently provides holistic financial planning for nearly 900 clients and tax preparation for approximately 500 clients, and manages over $3.5 billion in assets.

Greg's involvement in the financial planning and wealth management communities is well established. He is a member of the American Institute of Certified Public Accountants (AICPA) and the Financial Planning Association (FPA). In addition, he is a founding member of both the Alpha Group and Blind Squirrels, national consortia of wealth managers and business owners. He served as chairman (1996–1997), president (1995–1996), and on the board of directors (1989–1997) of the International Association for Financial Planning (now called the Financial Planning Association).

An avid skier, cyclist, and triathlete, Greg is the father of two grown children. He and his wife live in Alexandria, Virginia.

Visit Greg Sullivan at RetirementFail.com.

Resources

For information on financial therapy:

Financial Therapy Association: financialtherapyassociation.org

For additional information on or to report fraud:

Financial Industry Regulatory Authority: 844-57-HELPS hotline, or 844-574-3577 (established for older people to call if they have questions about their brokerage accounts, including statements and individual investments)

Identity Theft Resource Center: idtheftcenter.org

National Association of Attorneys General: www.naag.org

National Center on Elder Abuse (part of the federal Administration on Aging): www.ncea.aoa.gov

National Fraud Information Center: fraud.org

To report an IRS scam:

TIGTA (Treasury Inspector General for Tax Administration): 800-366-4484 treasury.gov/tigta/contact_report_scam.shtml

For questions about Medicare:

Medicare: 1-800-MEDICARE (1-800-633-4227), medicare.gov

SHIP (State Health Insurance Assistance Programs) National Technical Assistance Center (local help with Medicare and COBRA): https://www.shiptacenter.org/

Notes

INTRODUCTION

1. "Survey: Americans' Use of Financial Advisors, CFP Professionals Rises; Agree Advice Should Be in Their Best Interest," CFP Board, September 24, 2015, http://www.cfp.net/news-events/latest-news/2015/09/24/survey-americans-use-of-financial-advisors-cfp-professionals-rises-agree-advice-should-be-in-their-best-interest.

CHAPTER 1

1. Ruth Davis Konigsberg, "Beware the Retirement Splurge," *Time* magazine, November 23, 2015. Accessed June 18, 2017. http://time.com/money/4123785/retirement-spending/.
2. Konigsberg, "Beware the Retirement Splurge."
3. Money Habitudes, "Financial Statistics." Accessed September 15, 2017. http://www.moneyhabitudes.com/financial-statistics/.
4. Charlie Wells, "The Hidden Reasons People Spend Too Much," *Wall Street Journal,* November 2, 2105. Accessed June 23, 2017. https://www.wsj.com/articles/the-hidden-reasons-people-spend-too-much-1446433200.
5. "Actuarial Life Table," Social Security Administration. Accessed July 10, 2017. https://www.ssa.gov/oact/STATS/table4c6.html.
6. Sally Palaian, *Spent: Break the Buying Obsession and Discover Your True Worth* (Center City, Minnesota: Hazelden), 3.
7. Money Habitudes, "Financial Statistics." Accessed September 15, 2017. http://www.moneyhabitudes.com/financial-statistics/.

CHAPTER 2

1. Kathyrn Vasel, "It Costs $233,610 to Raise a Child," *CNN Money,* January 9, 2017. http://money.cnn.com/2017/01/09/pf/cost-of-raising-a-child-2015/.
2. "The Sandwich Generation: Rising Financial Burdens for Middle-Aged Americans," Pew Research Center, January 20, 2013. http://www.pewsocialtrends.org/2013/01/30/the-sandwich-generation/.
3. Money Habitudes, "Financial Statistics." Accessed September 22, 2017. http://www.moneyhabitudes.com/financial-statistics/.

4. "Fact Sheet: Focusing Higher Education on Student Success," U.S. Department of Education, July 27, 2015. https://www.ed.gov/news/press-releases/fact-sheet-focusing-higher-education-student-success.
5. Bella DePaulo, "Why Are So Many Young Adults Living with Their Parents?" *Psychology Today*, May 26, 2016. Accessed September 23, 2017. https://www.psychologytoday.com/blog/living-single/201605/why-are-so-many-young-adults-living-their-parents.

CHAPTER 3

1. Abby Ellin, "After Full Lives Together, More Older Couples Are Divorcing," *New York Times*, October 20, 2015. Accessed April 23, 2017. https://www.nytimes.com/2015/10/31/your-money/after-full-lives-together-more-older-couples-are-divorcing.html?_r=0.
2. Rob Stern, "Life Expectancy in U.S. Drops for First Time in Decades, Report Finds," *Morning Edition*, NPR, December 8, 2017. Accessed May 17, 2017. http://www.npr.org/sections/health-shots/2016/12/08/504667607/life-expectancy-in-u-s-drops-for-first-time-in-decades-report-finds.
3. Editorial staff, divorcesource.com, "Why Women File 80 Percent of Divorces," January 20, 2017. Accessed September 27, 2017. http://www.divorcesource.com/blog/why-women-file-80-percent-of-divorces/.
4. Susan Gregory Thomas, "The Gray Divorcés," *Wall Street Journal*, March 3, 2012. Accessed December 15, 2017. https://www.wsj.com/articles/SB10001424052970203753704577255230471480276.
5. Mark Banschick, "The High Failure Rate of Second and Third Marriages," *Psychology Today*, February 6, 2012. Accessed March 16, 2017. https://www.psychologytoday.com/blog/the-intelligent-divorce/201202/the-high-failure-rate-second-and-third-marriages.

CHAPTER 4

1. National Association of Realtors, *2015 NAR Investment and Vacation Home Buyers Survey*, April 2015. Accessed March 17, 2017. https://assets.documentcloud.org/documents/1699245/2015-nar-vacation-amp-investment-homes-survey.pdf.
2. National Association of Realtors, *2015 NAR Investment and Vacation Home Buyers Survey*, April 2015.
3. Adam DeSanctis, "Vacation Homes Soar to Record High in 2014, Investment Purchases Fall." National Association of Realtors press release, April 1, 2015. Accessed April 24, 2017. https://www.nar.realtor/news-releases/2015/04/vacation-home-sales-soar-to-record-high-in-2014-investment-purchases-fall.
4. Joanne Cleaver, "Why Your Vacation Home May Not Be Your Retirement Home, *U.S. News and World Report*, April 17, 2014. Accessed April 30, 2017. http://money.usnews.com/money/personal-finance/mutual-funds/articles/2014/04/17/why-your-vacation-home-may-not-be-your-retirement-home.

CHAPTER 5

1. Robert W. Fairlie, E. J. Reedy, Arnobio Morelix, and Joshua Russell, *The Kauffman 2016 Index of Startup Activity*, August 2016.
2. "Startup Business Failure Rate by Industry," Statistic Brain. Accessed June 21, 2017. http://www.statisticbrain.com/startup-failure-by-industry/.
3. Tom Anderson, "Employers Offer Older Workers Flexible Retirement," CNBC.com, August 21, 2016. Accessed June, 20, 2017. http://www.cnbc.com/2016/08/19/employers-offer-flexible-retirement-options-to-keep-older-workers.html.

CHAPTER 6

1. Laura Dimon and Graham Rayman, "State Supreme Court Judge Loses Over $1M in Real Estate Email Scam," *New York Daily News*, June 20, 2017. Accessed July 23, 2017. http://www.nydailynews.com/new-york/state-supreme-court-judge-loses-1m-real-estate-email-scam-article-1.3263091.
2. Javelin Research & Strategy, Press Release, *2017 Identity Fraud Study*, February 1, 2017. Accessed July 23, 2017. https://www.javelinstrategy.com/press-release/identity-fraud-hits-record-high-154-million-us-victims-2016-16-percent-according-new.
3. Kelly Phillips Erb, "Millennials Most Likely to Fall Victim to Tax & Financial Scams, *Forbes*, June 25, 2017. Accessed July 23, 2017. https://www.forbes.com/sites/kellyphillipserb/2017/06/25/millennials-most-likely-to-fall-victim-to-tax-financial-scams/#3651eb845353.
4. MetLife Mature Markets Institute, "Financial Abuse of Older Americans Has Increased Since 2008, According to the Latest Data from the Metlife Mature Market Institute," Mature Market News, June 2011. Accessed July 10, 2017. https://www.metlife.com/assets/cao/mmi/publications/mmi-pressroom/2011/mmi-elder-financial-abuse-pr.pdf.
5. TrueLink, "The TrueLink Report on Elder Financial Abuse 2015." Accessed July 23, 2017. https://www.truelinkfinancial.com/research.
6. True Link, "The True Link Report on Elder Financial Abuse 2015." Accessed July 23, 2017. https://www.truelinkfinancial.com/research.
7. Kevin McCoy, "Madoff Fund Has Paid Zero to Fraud Victims So Far," *USA Today*, May 23, 2017. Accessed July 23, 2017. https://www.usatoday.com/story/money/2017/05/23/us-madoff-fund-has-paid-zero-fraud-victims-so-far/102048186/.
8. National Adult Protective Services Association, "Elder Financial Exploitation" page. Accessed July 23, 2017. http://www.napsa-now.org/policy-advocacy/exploitation/.

CHAPTER 7

1. National Center for Health Statistics, *Health, United States, 2016: With Chartbook on Long-Term Trends in Health*, 2017 (p. 4). Accessed August 1, 2017. https://www.cdc.gov/nchs/data/hus/hus16.pdf#015.

2. National Center for Health Statistics, *Health, United States, 2016: With Chartbook on Long-Term Trends in Health,* 2017.
3. "Buying Long-Term Care Insurance," LongTermCare.gov, US Department of Health and Human Services. Accessed July 27, 2017. https://longtermcare.acl.gov/costs-how-to-pay/what-is-long-term -care-insurance/buying-long-term-care-insurance.html.
4. "How Much Care Will You Need?" LongTermCare.gov, US Department of Health and Human Services. Accessed July 27, 2017. https:// longtermcare.acl.gov/the-basics/how-much-care-will-you-need.html.
5. Kataliya Palmieri, "Exercise for Healthy Aging," adapted from a presentation for the Hospital for Special Surgery, April 7, 2004. Accessed August 1, 2017. https://www.hss.edu/conditions_exercise-healthy-aging.asp.
6. Harvard Health/Helpguide.org, "Sleep Tips for Older Adults," accessed July 31, 2017, https://www.helpguide.org/articles/sleep/how-to-sleep -well-as-you-age.htm#quality.
7. Harvard Health/Helpguide.org, "Sleep Tips for Older Adults."
8. "Facts About Aging and Alcohol," National Institute on Aging, U.S. Department of Health and Human Services, accessed July 30, 2017, https://www.nia.nih.gov/health/facts-about-aging-and-alcohol.

CHAPTER 8

1. Alicia R. Williams and S. Kathi Brown, "2017 Retirement Confidence Survey," AARP Research, December 2017. Accessed December 16, 2017. https://www.aarp.org/content/dam/aarp/research/surveys_statistics/ econ/2017/2017-retirement-confidence.doi.10.26419%252F.00174 .001.pdf.
2. "Death Vs. Disability – Which Is More Likely?" Financial Solutions Group, Inc. Accessed August 20, 2017. http://www.affordableinsurance protection.com/death_vs_disability.
3. "Disability Statistics," National Treasury Employees Union – Chapter 78. March 12, 2009.
4. "Disability Insurance Infographic," January 18, 2013. Accessed August 25, 2017. https://web.archive.org/web/20130123064308/ http://www .disabilityinsurance.org/articles/disability-insurance-infographic.html.
5. Insurance Research Council press release, "New Study Reveals a Declining Trend in the Percentage of Uninsured Motorists," August 5, 2014. Accessed August 18, 2017. http://www.insurance-research.org/ sites/default/files/downloads/IRC%20UM_NewsRelease_1.pdf.
6. "How Many Car Accidents Occur per Year?" Fetterman & Associates. Accessed August 20, 2017. http://www.lawteam.com/2015/07/27/how -many-car-accidents-occur-per-year/.

CHAPTER 9

1. Wells Fargo press release, "Wells Fargo Survey: Affluent Investors Feeling Good on Financial Health; Yet More Than Half Worry About Losing Money in the Market," July 15, 2015. Accessed August 18, 2017. https://newsroom.wf.com/press-release/community-banking-and -small-business/wells-fargo-survey-affluent-investors-feeling.
2. Money Habitudes, "Financial Statistics." Accessed September 22, 2017. http://www.moneyhabitudes.com/financial-statistics/.
3. Paulina Pchelin and Ryan T. Howell, "The Hidden Cost of Value-Seeking: People Do Not Accurately Forecast the Economic Benefits of Experiential Purchases," *The Journal of Positive Psychology* 9, No. 4 (March 2014). Accessed September 2, 2017. http://dx.doi.org/10.1080/17439760 .2014.898316.

Index

A

accidents, 134
advance directives, 109–110,
 111, 113
Affordable Care Act (ACA), 104,
 132
Alzheimer's disease, 105, 106
annual income need, 11, 12
annuities
financial fraud via, 89–91
 as income, 9
 long-term care insurance
 and, 108
appraisers, 47
asset allocation, 9, 11–12
assets
 illiquid, 45, 61
 liability insurance and, 125
 lifestyle vs. investment, 60–64,
 68
 liquid, 61
 prenuptial agreements and,
 51–53
 splitting in divorce, 42–49
 theft of, 92–94
 titling of, 54
 valuation of, 45–47, 49
 See also specific types
auto insurance, 125, 126
avoiders (money personality),
 137

B

bank accounts
 in divorce settlements, 45
 power of attorney and, 110
 scams and, 91, 93–94, 95
bankruptcy, 2
Barron's, 145
Beatty, Diane, 125
behavioral issues
 family spending and, 33–34
 overspending as, 15–16,
 18, 19
 prenuptial agreements and,
 52
beneficiaries, documentation of,
 124
Blayney, Eleanor, xv, 76
bonds, 12, 61
Bredesen, Dale, 106
Bruyette, Jim, xiv, 19, 76, 79
budgets, 18
business debt, in divorce
 settlements, 44
businesses
 as assets in divorce, 45, 47, 49
 financial advisor expertise for,
 147
 start-ups, 71–79, 83–84
business partnerships, 75–76, 80
business plans for start-ups,
 71–76, 79, 83

C

CAL Insurance & Associates, 125, 126
car loans, in divorce settlements, 44
cash flow
    during divorce proceedings, 50
    early retirement and, 116
    in vs. out, 15
certificates of deposit (CDs), 12, 61
Certified Financial Planner (CFP)
    expertise level of, 146
    for fraud detection, 96
    insurance advice from, 90
    tax advice from, 47
certified public accountants (CPAs)
    as career, xiv
    expertise level of, 146
    tax advice from, 47
charitable contributions
    overspending on, 16–17
    tax implications of, 124
Chartered Financial Analyst (CFA), 146
children
    as beneficiaries, 124
    divorce and, 38, 39, 48, 53
    as entrepreneurs, 77–79
    failure to launch, 26–34
    financial decisions involving, 5–6
    in financial plan, 7, 132
    funding education of, 23–25
    gifts to, 35, 140–142
    health insurance for, 104
    life circumstances of, 25–26

life insurance and, 120–122
marriage of, 54
from previous marriages, 45
supporting special-needs, 22–23, 26, 132–134, 135
child support, 51
closing costs, 57, 58, 59, 63–64, 68
COBRA health insurance, 103
cognitive decline, 112, 119
computer malware, 95
consulting businesses, 81, 82, 116
credit agencies, 96
credit card debt, in divorce settlements, 44
credit card fraud, 94–96
Cristobal, Virg, 108, 123
Cristobal Associates/Sagemark Consulting, 108, 123

D

death, leading causes of, 100
debit card fraud, 95
debt, in divorce settlements, 44, 48
defined benefit plans, 46.
    See also pension plans
defined contribution plans, 49
disability. *See* illness/disability
disability insurance, 105, 116, 118–119, 134
diversification, 130, 132
dividends from retirement portfolios, 12
divorce
    financial advisors and, 39–42
    life insurance and, 122
    long-term health care and, 107

no-fault, 44
outcome of, 53
rate of, 37
remarriage and, 50–51
in retirement years, 37–38
splitting assets in, 42–49,
    51–53
Dondero, Dave, xiv
downsizing
    postdivorce, 53
    in retirement plan, 16, 19
    to support children, 26
dual authentication, 95
durable power of attorney, 109

E
earning potential, in divorce
    settlements, 47–48
economic downturn
    fear of, 139
    preparing for, 127–129, 135
    See also financial crisis of
        2008–2009
education
    as financial strain, 20, 22,
        23–25
    risk tolerance and, 11
elder abuse, 93
e-mail scams, 85, 91, 94–95, 98
emergencies, planning for, 18
employment
    long-term care insurance and,
        106
    loss of, 114–118
    Medicare and, 102–103
    phasing into retirement from,
        81
    during retirement, 19, 28,
        81–83
    spending habits and, 3

Employment Retirement
    Income Security Act
    (ERISA), 48
The End of Alzheimer's
    (Bredesen), 106
entrepreneurs
    helping your children
        become, 77–79
    retirees as, 69–71, 80, 83–84
    skills needed by, 72, 73–74,
        79–80
    See also start-up businesses
Equifax, 96
Ernst & Whinney (now Ernst &
    Young), xiv, 118
estate planning
    advance directives in, 109–110
    divorce and, 40, 50
    documentation for, 124
    life insurance in, 123, 135
    prenuptial agreements and,
        53
estate tax, 123
expenses
    age and, 13
    children as, 21
    in financial plan
        development, 18
    necessary, 17, 34
    unexpected, 7–8
Experian, 96
expertise
    of financial advisors, 146
    of retirees, 83

F
failure to launch, 26–34
family
    attitudes toward money in,
        137

family (*continued*)
  financial advisor relationship with, 145
  gifts to, 140–142
  planning for unexpected events in, 132–134, 135
  See also children; spouses
family-owned businesses
  as assets in divorce, 45, 47, 49
  as start-ups, 77–79
  stock from, 130
fault divorce, 44, 48
Fidelity, 96
Financial Advisor, xi, xii
financial advisors
  advance directives and, 110
  for business start-ups, 74, 76, 79–80
  careers as, xiv
  checklist for, 149–150
  divorce settlements and, 40, 54
  fees charged by, 147–148
  finding, 144–150
  for fraud detection, 90–91, 92, 96, 97
  insurance policies and, 135
  percent of investors working with, xiii
  for planning retirement expenses, 7, 142–143
  prenuptial agreements and, 52
  real estate investment schemes and, 89
  second home purchases and, 56, 61, 65
  setting retirement goals and, 29
  trust setup and, 23
financial crisis of 2008–2009, 21, 62, 63, 78, 114–115, 117
financial decisions
  by adult children, 27, 31
  advance directives for, 109–110
  determining risk level in, 9, 11
  by entrepreneurs, 73
  evaluating impact of, 8
  funnel approach to, 9, *10*, 111
  informed, 6, 18
  to prevent exploitation, 94
  on second homes, 60, 62–63, 65–68
  spouses and, 139
  on supporting children, 29
  unexpected events and, 134
financial documentation
  ensuring access to, 124
  fraud detection and, 97
financial exploitation, 92–94
financial fraud
  in annuities/financial products, 89–90
  by family members, 87
  incidence of, 85
  via phone/Internet, 91–92
  Ponzi schemes as, 87–88
  protection from, 94–98
  in real estate, 88–89
  reporting, 98
  targets of, 86–87
financial independence
  of children, 21–22, 26–35, 39
  divorce and, 50
  in retirement, 9, 12
  start-up businesses and, 71
  unexpected events and, 115, 117
  for women, 38

Financial Industry Regulatory
    Authority (FINRA), 98
financial plan
    developing, 18
    in divorce, 50
    expenses included in, 7
    setting priorities in, 29
    support for disabled children
        in, 22
Fitch, 90
529 plans, 24
Forbes, 145
401(k) plans
    as assets in divorce, 46–47, 49
    early retirement and, 116
funnel approach, 9

G
gender
    financial independence and,
        38
    financial support of children
        and, 22
    views of wealth and, 147
gifts
    to children, 35, 140–142
    divorce and, 43, 45
    spending on, 143
Google, 131
grandchildren, support of, 25,
    133
Great Recession. *See* financial
    crisis of 2008–2009
growth assets, 12

H
health care
    advance directives for,
        109–110, 111
    aging and, 111–113

for children, 22–23, 28
expenses for, 13
personal views about, 101
as retirement disruptor, 99,
    100
See also long-term care (LTC)
    insurance
health insurance, 100, 101–104,
    116
hobbies, overspending and,
    13–15
homes
    as assets in divorce, 45–46, 48
    costs associated with, 57–58
    valuations of, 59
    See also second homes

I
identity
    as entrepreneur, 70
    maintaining in retirement,
        17, 82
identity fraud, 85, 91–92,
    94–96
Identity Guard, 96
identity protection services, 96
illiquid assets, 45, 61
illness/disability
    as divorce settlement
        consideration, 47
    early retirement and,
        115–116, 118–119
    financial exploitation and, 93
    as financial strain, 22, 102,
        121–122
    long-term care for, 104–109
    preparing for, 99, 100,
        110–111, 126, 134
income
    college education and, 23

income (*continued*)
  as financial plan
      consideration, 8–9
  phased retirement and, 81
  preretirement, 3
  working during retirement as,
      19, 71
individual retirement accounts
      (IRAs)
  as assets in divorce, 46
  early retirement and, 116
Ingram, Gary, 23, 41
inheritance
  divorce and, 43
  equalizing, 123–124
  planning for, 140–142
  trusts and, 23
Inside Retirement conference,
      xii
insurance policies
  auto, 125, 126
  disability, 105, 134
  in divorce settlements, 50, 51
  fraud and, 90, 93
  health, 100, 101–104, 113
  life, 40, 81, 90, 108, 120–124
  long-term care, 104–109, 113
  phased retirement and, 81
  for second homes, 57, 59
  umbrella, 125–127
  unexpected events and, 115,
      134, 135
interest on retirement
      portfolio, 12
Internal Revenue Service (IRS),
      46–47, 91–92
investment portfolio
  building, 9–13
  diversification in, 130, 132
  divorce and, 42–49

  early retirement and, 116
  economic downturns and,
      127–129, 135
  as income, 8, 9
  performance of, 4, 12
  progressive illness and, 111
  vs. real estate investments, 60
  third-party custodians for,
      96, 97
  withdrawals from, 8–9, 13
investment risk, 9, 11
investment strategy, 12, 111,
      114, 130, 146

J
Jacobs, Stafford, 126
joint property, 44–45, 48

K
Katz, Jon, 102–104, 121, 122

L
layoffs, 114–118
Lehman Brothers, 131
liability insurance, 125–127
life changes as financial
      strain, 22
life expectancy, 13, 38, 105
life insurance, 40, 81, 90, 108,
      120–124, 135
LifeLock, 96
life purpose
  fulfillment and, 38
  in retirement years, 17
  work and, 83
lifestyle
  affordable, 1, 2, 18
  divorce and, 42
  generating income to
      support, 5

healthy, 111–113
  second homes and, 60–64, 68
limited liability companies
      (LLCs), 75
limited partnerships, 61
liquid assets, 61
living will, 109, 110, 111, 113
loans
  to children, 20–21, 30–31, 32,
      35
  in divorce settlements, 44
long-term care (LTC) insurance,
      104–108
lottery scams, 92
low-risk assets, 12

M
Madoff, Bernie, 87, 88, 96
Medicaid, 133
Medicare, 102–104, 116, 133
Medicare Advantage, 104
Microsoft, 130
Millennials, financial fraud and,
      86
money, attitudes toward,
      136–143
Moody's, 90
Morningstar, 97
mortgages
  in divorce settlements,
      44, 48
  interest rates for, 58
  shared ownership and, 67
mutual funds, 61

N
Natovitz, Kim, 107
Natovitz Group, 107
natural disasters, 65–66
necessary spending, 17

no-fault divorce, 44
nonprofit work, 81, 82

O
Obamacare (ACA), 104, 132
operating agreements for
      start-ups, 75–76
overspending, 2–3, 13–19. *See
      also* spending habits
own-occupation disability
      insurance, 118–119, 134

P
partnership agreements,
      72, 75, 76
passions
  overspending and, 13–15
  pursuing, 19
passwords, 95
Patient Protection and
      Affordable Care Act
      (ACA), 104, 132
pension plans
  as assets in divorce, 46, 49
  death of spouse and, 16
  early retirement and, 116
  as income, 8, 9
permanent life insurance,
      122–123
Pershing, 96
personal financial management,
      4
phishing scams, 85, 91–92
phone scams, 91–92, 94
Ponzi schemes, 87–88, 96–97
power of attorney (POA), 109,
      110, 111, 113
prenuptial/postnuptial
      agreements, 45,
      51–53, 54

preretirement income, 3
private equities
  fraud detection and, 97
  as illiquid assets, 61
  in investment portfolio, 12
property, joint vs. sole, 44–45, 46
property agreements, 48
property taxes, 46, 58
property values, 46, 59, 68
pyramid schemes, 87–88

Q
qualified domestic relations
    order (QDRO), 48–49

R
real estate
  as asset in divorce, 44
  as illiquid asset, 61
  as investment, 12, 57–60, 63
  investment fraud in, 88–89
  See also homes; second homes
remarriage
  divorce rate and, 50–51
  financial documentation and,
    124
rental properties, 67
required minimum
    distributions, 46–47
retirement
  boredom in, 69–71, 72, 80, 81
  disruptors of, 115–135
  early, 115–118
  employment during, 19, 28,
    81–83
  entrepreneurship during,
    69–71, 80
  financial funnels for, 9, *10*
  fraud incidence and, 86, 90
  goals for, 2, 6, 7–9, 29

health-care disruptions of, 99,
    100
  isolation in, 112
  low-risk start-ups in, 81–82
  phased, 80–81
  rate of, xii
  second homes and, 55–56
  spending habits in, 3, 9,
    137–143
retirement accounts
  as assets in divorce, 44, 45, 46,
    48–49
  documentation for, 124
  early retirement and, 116
  See also investment portfolio
retirement homes, 64–65
return on investment
  economic downturns and,
    127–129
  financial fraud and, 96, 97
  from real estate, 59–60, 68, 89
  from retirement portfolio, 9
risk
  in business start-ups, 73, 74,
    76–77
  extreme frugality and,
    138–139
  in investing, 9, 11
  long-term health care and,
    108
  in real estate schemes, 88
  with single stocks, 129–132
  tolerance for, 11

S
salary, in income funnel, 9
savers (money personality), 137
scams. *See* financial fraud
Schelhorn, Barbara, 27–28
Schepis, Pam, 58

Schwab, 96
second homes
   as investments, 57–60, 68
   justifications for, 55–56
   as lifestyle assets, 60–64
   natural disasters and, 65–66
   partial ownership of, 66–67
   renting vs. buying, 57, 60, 64
   for retirement living, 64–65
Securities and Exchange
     Commission (SEC), 97,
     98
Security Analysis (Graham), 11
self-employment, 71
senior citizens
   financial exploitation of,
     92–94
   financial fraud and, 86–92
Sharper Image, 131
Simonoff, Evan, xii
skimmers, 95
Social Security
   death of spouse and, 16
   early retirement and, 116
   as income, 8, 9
   Medicare and, 102
   special-needs children and,
     133
Social Security Administration,
     13
spenders (money personality),
     137
spending habits
   affordable risk and, 9
   age and, 13
   control of, 1–2, 13–19
   early retirement and,
     117–118
   extreme frugality as, 138,
     139–140

family patterns of, 33–34
   primary income source and, 9
   as retirement fail cause,
     2, 137
   second homes and, 58, 68
   sources of, 4–7
   between spouses, 5–6, 15–16
   during working years vs.
     retirement, 3–4
Speros, Pete, xiv–xv, 76
spousal support, 49, 51
spouses
   as beneficiaries, 124
   health-care crises and, 100
   hiding spending from, 15
   life insurance and, 120–122,
     135
   money personalities of, 5, 16,
     139–140, 143
   prenuptial agreements for, 45,
     51–53
   See also divorce; joint
     property; remarriage
Standard & Poor's, 90
start-up businesses
   failures of, 78, 83
   financial advice for, 79–80
   helping family with, 77–79
   low-risk, for retirees, 81–82
   operating agreement for,
     75–76
   plan for, 71–75, 79
   risk with, 76–77
stock market
   spending rates and, 13
   tech bubble in, 129, 130
   volatility of, 12, 65, 129
stocks
   in divorce settlements, 45
   economic downturns and, 128

stocks (*continued*)
in investment portfolio, 11, 12
as liquid assets, 61
risks with, 129–132
student loans, in divorce
settlements, 44
Sullivan, Bruyette, Speros &
Blayney (SBSB), xii, 19,
27, 76, 145
Sullivan Financial Consultants,
xiv

T
taxes
disability insurance and, 119
divorce and, 50, 54
estate, 123
estate planning and, 124
financial advisor expertise
and, 147
529 plans and, 24
life insurance and, 122
on real estate, 46, 58
on retirement accounts,
46–47
second homes and, 57
TD Ameritrade, 96
term life insurance, 122–123

third-party custodians for
investment accounts, 96,
97
TransUnion, 96
Tribridge Partners, 107
trusts
estate taxes and, 123
to support children, 23, 30,
31, 124, 133–134

U
umbrella insurance, 125–127
unemployment benefits, 116

V
vacation homes. *See* second
homes
Vanguard, 96
Virginia Medical Plans/Katz
Insurance Group, 102,
121

W
Washingtonian, 145
wealth
children as drain on, 21
underliving, 136–143
work. *See* employment